Lambert M. Surhone, Mariam T. Tennoe,
Susan F. Henssonow (Ed.)

Colville-Okanagan Language

Lambert M. Surhone, Mariam T. Tennoe,
Susan F. Henssonow (Ed.)

Colville-Okanagan Language

International Phonetic Alphabet, Salishan Languages

Betascript Publishing

Imprint

Permission is granted to copy, distribute and/or modify this document under the terms of the GNU Free Documentation License, Version 1.2 or any later version published by the Free Software Foundation; with no Invariant Sections, with the Front-Cover Texts, and with the Back-Cover Texts. A copy of the license is included in the section entitled "GNU Free Documentation License".

All parts of this book are extracted from Wikipedia, the free encyclopedia (www.wikipedia.org).

You can get detailed informations about the authors of this collection of articles at the end of this book. The editors (Ed.) of this book are no authors. They have not modified or extended the original texts.

Pictures published in this book can be under different licences than the GNU Free Documentation License. You can get detailed informations about the authors and licences of pictures at the end of this book.

The content of this book was generated collaboratively by volunteers. Please be advised that nothing found here has necessarily been reviewed by people with the expertise required to provide you with complete, accurate or reliable information. Some information in this book maybe misleading or wrong. The Publisher does not guarantee the validity of the information found here. If you need specific advice (f.e. in fields of medical, legal, financial, or risk management questions) please contact a professional who is licensed or knowledgeable in that area.

Any brand names and product names mentioned in this book are subject to trademark, brand or patent protection and are trademarks or registered trademarks of their respective holders. The use of brand names, product names, common names, trade names, product descriptions etc. even without a particular marking in this works is in no way to be construed to mean that such names may be regarded as unrestricted in respect of trademark and brand protection legislation and could thus be used by anyone.

Cover image: www.ingimage.com
Concerning the licence of the cover image please contact ingimage.

Contact:
VDM Publishing House Ltd.,17 Rue Meldrum, Beau Bassin,1713-01 Mauritius
Email: info@vdm-publishing-house.com
Website: www.vdm-publishing-house.com

Published in 2010
Printed in: U.S.A., U.K., Germany. This book was not produced in Mauritius.

ISBN: 978-613-2-39665-5

Contents

Articles

References

Article Licenses

Colville-Okanagan language

Colville-Okanagan	
nsəlxcin	
Spoken in	Canada, United States of America
Region	Southern Interior of British Columbia, Central-northern State of Washington
Total speakers	200

Language family	Salishan
	• Interior Salish
	  • Southern
	    • Colville-Okanagan

Language codes	
ISO 639-1	*None*
ISO 639-2	–
ISO 639-3	oka [1]

The **Colville-Okanagan** language, known to its speakers as *nsəlxcin* or *nsyilxcn*, is the traditional language of the Lower Similkameen Indian Band, the Upper Similkameen Indian Band, the Westbank First Nation, the Osoyoos Indian Band, the Penticton Indian Band, the Okanagan Indian Band, the Upper Nicola Indian Band, and the Colville, Sanpoil, Okanogan, Lakes, Nespelem and Methow bands of the Confederated Tribes of the Colville Reservation. Colville-Okanagan is a member of the Interior Salish group of Salishan languages.

Historically, Colville-Okanagan originated from a language, now termed Proto-Salish, which was spoken in the lower Fraser River between 4000 BCE and 1000 BCE. As speakers of Proto-Salish spread across the Pacific Northwest the language fragmented and developed into the modern Salishan languages including Colville-Okanagan. Speakers of *nsəlxcin* occupied the northern portion of the Columbia Basin from the Methow River in the west, to Kootenay Lake in the east, and north along the Columbia River until the site of what is now the present day city of Golden.

There are three separate Colville-Okanagan dialects: Colville, Okanagan, and Lakes. There is a low degree of dialectic divergence making cross-dialect communication relatively easy.

There are currently about 200 fluent speakers of Colville-Okanagan Salish with the majority of speakers living in British Columbia. The language is currently moribund and has no fluent speakers younger than 50 years of age.

Colville-Okanagan was an exclusively oral form of communication until the late 1800s when linguists began transcribing the language for word lists, dictionaries, and grammars. Cv-Ok is primarily written using the International Phonetic Alphabet. Salish literacy is widespread but incomplete among current speakers.

Okanagan is reported to contain the rare uvular flap.[2]

See also

- Okanagan people
- Okanagan Nation Alliance

Further reading

- Anstey, Robert G. *Okanagan Poems: Kelowna, Vernon, Peachland, Keremeos, Summerland, Westbank, Penticton : Souvenir Book : Poetry*. Vernon, B.C.: West Coast Paradise Pub, 1996.
- Doak, Ivy G. *The 1908 Okanagan Word Lists of James Teit*. Missoula, Montana: Dept. of Anthropology, University of Montana, 1983.
- Dubeta, John C. *Writers of the Okanagan Mainline*. Kelowna, B.C.: Okanagan Mainline Senior Writers' and Publishers' Association, 1985. ISBN 0969207905
- Mattina, Anthony. *Colville-Okanagan Dictionary*. Missoula, Mont: Dept. of Anthropology, University of Montana, 1987.
- Mattina, Nancy J. *Aspect and Category in Okanagan Word Formation*. Ottawa: National Library of Canada = Bibliothèque nationale du Canada, 1997. ISBN 061217011X
- Nybo, Darcy. *Okanagan Tales: Stories from the Okanagan in Beautiful British Columbia*. Westbank, BC: Chameleon Communications, 2004. ISBN 0968169414
- Pryce, Elizabeth. *Skaha Crossing: An Okanagan Story : Historical Fiction Novel*. Victoria, B.C.: Trafford, 2004. ISBN 1412037859
- Smith, Penny, and Yasmin John-Thorpe. *Gems of the Okanagan, 2006: Volume One : Poems and Short Stories*. Penticton, B.C.: Penticton Writers and Publishers, 2006. ISBN 0969844972
- *South Okanagan Anthology*. Penticton, B.C.: Theytus Books, 1984. ISBN 0919441203
- Kuipers, Aert H. (2002). *Salish Etymological Dictionary*. UMOPL No.16. ISBN 1-879763-16-8.
- Swadesh, Morris. (1950). *Salish Internal Relationships*. International Journal of American Linguistics, 16, 157-167.
- Kroever, Paul D. (1999). *The Salish Language Family: Reconstructing Syntax*.
- Kinkade, Dale. M. (1990). *Prehistory of Salishan languages*.
- Peterson, Sarah, with Wiley, Larae, and Parkin, Christopher (2004) *Nsəlxcin 1, Nsəlxcin 2, Nsəlxcin 3, Captík^{w}ɬ 1, Captík^{w}ɬ 2, Captík^{w}ɬ 3*

External links

- Colville-Okanagan language [3] at Ethnologue
- Colville-Okanagan language [4] at LINGUIST List
- First Nations Languages of British Columbia entry [5]
- Map of Northwest Coast First Nations [6]
- Vocabulary Words in Okanagan-Colville [7]
- Salish School of Spokane [8]

References

[1] http://www.sil.org/iso639-3/documentation.asp?id=oka

[2] "Uvular-Pharyngeal Resonants in Interior Salish." M. Dale Kinkade. International Journal of American Linguistics, Vol. 33, No. 3 (Jul., 1967), pp. 228–234

[3] http://www.ethnologue.org/show_language.asp?code=oka

[4] http://linguistlist.org/forms/langs/LLDescription.cfm?code=oka

[5] http://www.ydli.org/langs/okanagan.htm

[6] http://www.bced.gov.bc.ca/abed/images/map2.jpg

[7] http://www.native-languages.org/okanagan_words.htm

[8] http://www.salishschoolofspokane.org/?home

International Phonetic Alphabet

International Phonetic Alphabet	
[aɪ pʰiː eɪ]	
Type	Partially featural alphabet
Spoken languages	Used for phonetic and phonemic transcription of any language
Time period	since 1888
Parent systems	Romic alphabet • Phonotypic alphabet • International Phonetic Alphabet
Note: This page may contain IPA phonetic symbols.	

The **International Phonetic Alphabet (IPA)**[1] is a system of phonetic notation based primarily on the Latin alphabet, devised by the International Phonetic Association as a standardized representation of the sounds of spoken language.[2] The IPA is used by foreign language students and teachers, linguists, speech pathologists and therapists, singers, actors, lexicographers, conlangers and translators.[3] [4]

The IPA is designed to represent only those qualities of speech that are distinctive in spoken language: phonemes, intonation, and the separation of words and syllables.[2] To represent additional qualities of speech such as tooth gnashing, lisping, and sounds made with a cleft palate, an extended set of symbols called the Extensions to the IPA is used.[3]

Occasionally symbols are added, removed, or modified by the International Phonetic Association. As of 2008, there are 107 distinct letters, 52 diacritics, and four prosody marks in the IPA proper.

History

In 1886, a group of French and British language teachers, led by the French linguist Paul Passy, formed what would come to be known (from 1897 onwards) as the International Phonetic Association (in French, *l'Association phonétique internationale*).[5] The original alphabet was based on a spelling reform for English known as the Romic alphabet, but in order to make it usable for other languages, the values of the symbols were allowed to vary from language to language.[6] For example, the sound [ʃ] (the *sh* in *shoe*) was originally represented with the letter ‹c› in English, but with the letter ‹x› in French.[5] However, in 1888, the alphabet was revised so as to be uniform across languages, thus providing the base for all future revisions.[5] [7]

Since its creation, the IPA has undergone a number of revisions. After major revisions and expansions in 1900 and 1932, the IPA remained unchanged until the IPA Kiel Convention in 1989. A minor revision took place in 1993, with the addition of four mid-central vowels[3] and the removal of symbols for voiceless implosives.[8] The alphabet was last revised in May 2005, with the addition of a symbol for the labiodental flap.[9] Apart from the addition and removal of symbols, changes to the IPA have consisted largely in renaming symbols and categories and modifying typefaces.[3]

Extensions of the alphabet are relatively recent; "Extensions to the IPA" was created in 1990 and officially adopted by the International Clinical Phonetics and Linguistics Association in 1994.[10]

Description

The general principle of the IPA is to provide one symbol for each distinctive sound (or speech segment).[11] This means that it does not use letter combinations to represent single sounds,[12] or single letters to represent multiple sounds (the way ‹x› represents [ks] or [gz] in English). There are no letters that have context-dependent sound values (as ‹c› does in English and other European languages), and finally, the IPA does not usually have separate letters for two sounds if no known language makes a distinction between them (a property known as "selectiveness"[3]).[13]

Among the symbols of the IPA, 107 represent consonants and vowels, 31 are diacritics that are used to further specify these sounds, and 19 are used to indicate such qualities as length, tone, stress, and intonation.[14]

THE INTERNATIONAL PHONETIC ALPHABET (2005)

A chart of the full International Phonetic Alphabet.

Letterforms

The symbols chosen for the IPA are meant to harmonize with the Latin alphabet.[15] For this reason, most symbols are either Latin or Greek letters, or modifications thereof. However, there are symbols that are neither: for example, the symbol denoting the glottal stop, ‹ʔ›, has the form of a "gelded" question mark, and was originally an apostrophe.[16] In fact, there are a few symbols, such as that of the voiced pharyngeal fricative, ‹ʕ›, which, though modified to blend with the Latin alphabet, were inspired by glyphs in other writing systems (in this case, the Arabic letter ع, ʿain).[8]

Despite its preference for letters that harmonize with the Latin alphabet, the International Phonetic Association has occasionally admitted symbols that do not have this property. For example, before 1989, the IPA symbols for click consonants were ‹ʘ›, ⟨ʇ⟩, ‹ʗ›, and ‹ʖ›, all of which were derived either from existing symbols, or from Latin and Greek letters. However, except for ‹ʘ›, none of these symbols was widely used among Khoisanists or Bantuists, and as a result they were replaced by the more widespread symbols ‹ʘ›, ⟨ǀ⟩, ⟨ǃ⟩, ‹ǂ›, and ⟨ǁ⟩ at the IPA Kiel Convention in 1989.[17]

Some of the new symbols were ordinary Roman letters typeset "turned" (= upside-down) (e.g. ʎ ɥ ə ɔ ɹ), which was easily done before mechanical typesetting machines came into use.

Symbols and sounds

The International Phonetic Alphabet is based on the Latin alphabet, using as few non-Latin forms as possible.[] The Association created the IPA so that the sound values of most consonants taken from the Latin alphabet would correspond to "international usage".[] Hence, the letters ‹b›, ‹d›, ‹f›, (hard) ‹g›, (non-silent) ‹h›, (unaspirated) ‹k›, ‹l›, ‹m›, ‹n›, (unaspirated) ‹p›, (voiceless) ‹s›, (unaspirated) ‹t›, ‹v›, ‹w›, and ‹z› have the values used in English; and the vowels from the Latin alphabet (‹a›, ‹e›, ‹i›, ‹o›, ‹u›) correspond to the sound values of Latin: [i] is like the vowel in *machine*, [u] is as in *rule*, etc. Other letters may differ from English, but are used with these values in other European languages, such as ‹j›, ‹r›, and ‹y›.

This inventory was extended by using capital or cursive forms, diacritics, and rotation. There are also several derived or taken from the Greek alphabet, though the sound values may differ. For example, ‹ʊ› is a vowel in Greek, but an only indirectly related consonant in the IPA. Two of these (‹θ› and ‹χ›) are used unmodified in form; for others (including ‹β›, ‹γ›, ‹ɛ›, ‹ɸ›, and ‹ʊ›) subtly different glyph shapes have been devised, which may be encoded in Unicode separately from their "parent" letters.

The sound values of modified Latin letters can often be derived from those of the original letters.[18] For example, letters with a rightward-facing hook at the bottom represent retroflex consonants; and small capital letters usually represent uvular consonants. Apart from the fact that certain kinds of modification to the shape of a letter generally correspond to certain kinds of modification to the sound represented, there is no way to deduce the sound represented by a symbol from the shape of the symbol (unlike, for example, in Visible Speech).

Beyond the letters themselves, there are a variety of secondary symbols which aid in transcription. Diacritic marks can be combined with IPA letters to transcribe modified phonetic values or secondary articulations. There are also special symbols for suprasegmental features such as stress and tone that are often employed.

Brackets and phonemes

There are two principal types of brackets used to set off IPA transcriptions:

- [square brackets] are used for phonetic details of the pronunciation, possibly including details that may not be used for distinguishing words in the language being transcribed, but which the author nonetheless wishes to document.
- /slashes/ are used to mark off phonemes, all of which are distinctive in the language, without any extraneous detail.

For example, while the /p/ sounds of *pin* and *spin* are pronounced slightly differently in English (and this difference would be meaningful in some languages), it is not meaningful in English. Thus *phonemically* the words are /pɪn/ and /spɪn/, with the same /p/ phoneme. However, to capture the difference between them (the allophones of /p/), they can be transcribed phonetically as [pʰɪn] and [spɪn].

Two other conventions are less commonly seen:

- Double slashes, //...//, pipes, |...|, double pipes, ‖...‖, or braces, {...}, may be used around a word to denote its underlying structure, more abstract even than that of phonemes. See morphophonology for examples.
- Angle brackets are used to clarify that the letters represent the original orthography of the language, or sometimes an exact transliteration of a non-Latin script, not the IPA; or, within the IPA, that the letters themselves are indicated, not the sound values that they carry. For example, ‹pin› and ‹spin› would be seen for those words, which do not contain the *ee* sound [i] of the IPA letter ‹i›. Italics are perhaps more commonly used for this purpose when full words are being written (as *pin, spin* above), but this convention may not be considered sufficiently clear for individual letters and digraphs. The true angle brackets, ... (U+27E8, U+29E9), are not supported by many non-mathematical fonts as of 2010. Therefore chevrons, ‹...› (U+2039, U+203A), are sometimes used in substitution, as are the less-than and greater-than signs, <...> (U+003C, U+003E).

Usage

[eboʃ]

Ébauche is a French term meaning *outline* or *blank*.

Although the IPA offers over a hundred symbols for transcribing speech, it is not necessary to use all relevant symbols at the same time; it is possible to transcribe speech with various levels of precision. A precise phonetic transcription, in which sounds are described in a great deal of detail, is known as a *narrow transcription*. A coarser transcription which ignores some of this detail is called a *broad transcription*. Both are relative terms, and both are generally enclosed in square brackets.[] Broad phonetic transcriptions may restrict themselves to easily heard details, or only to details that are relevant to the discussion at hand, and may differ little if at all from phonemic transcriptions, but they make no theoretical claim that all the distinctions transcribed are necessarily meaningful in the language.

For example, the English word *little* may be transcribed broadly using the IPA as ['lɪtəl], and this broad (imprecise) transcription is an accurate (approximately correct) description of many pronunciations. A more narrow transcription may focus on individual or dialectical details: ['ɬɪɾɬ] in General American, ['lɪʔo] in Cockney, or ['ɬɪːɬ] in Southern US English.

$$[\text{ɪntə}^\text{ˈ}\text{næʃənəɫ}]$$
$$[\text{ɪɾ̃ɚ}^\text{ˈ}\text{næʃɨnəɫ}]$$

Phonetic transcriptions of the word *international* in two English dialects. The square brackets indicate that the differences between these dialects are not necessarily sufficient to distinguish different words in English.

It is customary to use simpler letters, without a lot of diacritics, in phonemic transcriptions. The choice of IPA letters may reflect the theoretical claims of the author, or merely be a convenience for typesetting. For instance, in English, either the vowel of *pick* or the vowel of *peak* may be transcribed as /i/ (for the pairs /pik, piːk/ or /pɪk, pik/), and neither is identical to the vowel of the French word *pique* which is also generally transcribed /i/. That is, letters between slashes do not have absolute values, something true of broader phonetic approximations as well. A narrow transcription may, however, be used to distinguish them: [pʰɪk], [pʰiːk], [pik].

Linguists

Although IPA is popular for transcription by linguists, it is also common to use Americanist phonetic notation or IPA together with some nonstandard symbols, for reasons including reducing the error rate on reading handwritten transcriptions or avoiding perceived awkwardness of IPA in some situations. The exact practice may vary somewhat between languages and even individual researchers, so authors are generally encouraged to include a chart or other explanation of their choices.[19]

Language study

Some language study programs use the IPA to teach pronunciation. For example, in Russia (and earlier in the Soviet Union), mainland China, and in Taiwan textbooks for children[20] and adults[21] for studying English and French consistently use the IPA.

Dictionaries

English

Many British dictionaries, among which are learner's dictionaries such as the Oxford Advanced Learner's Dictionary and the Cambridge Advanced Learner's Dictionary, now use the International Phonetic Alphabet to represent the pronunciation of words.[22] However, most American (and some British) volumes use one of a variety of pronunciation respelling systems, intended to be more comfortable for readers of English. For example, the respelling systems in many American dictionaries (such as Merriam–Webster) use ‹y› for IPA [j] and ‹sh› for IPA [ʃ], reflecting common representations of those sounds in written English,[23] using only letters of the English Roman alphabet and variations of them. (In IPA, [y] represents the sound of the French ‹u› (as in *tu*), and [sh] represents the pair of sounds in *grasshopper*.)

One of the benefits of using an alternative to the IPA is the ability to use a single symbol for a sound pronounced differently in different dialects. For example, The American Heritage Dictionary of the English Language uses ‹ŏ› for the vowel in *cot* (kŏt) [24] but ‹ô› for the one in *caught* (kôt) [25],[26] Some American speakers pronounce these the same way (for example, like IPA [ɒ] in the Boston dialect); for those speakers who maintain the distinction, depending on the accent, the vowel in *cot* may vary from [ɑ] to [a], while the vowel in *caught* may vary from [ɔ] to [ɑ], or may even be a diphthong. Using one symbol for the vowel in *cot* (instead of having different symbols for different pronunciations of the *o*) enables the dictionary to provide meaningful pronunciations for speakers of most dialects of English.

Other languages

The IPA is also not universal among dictionaries in languages other than English. Monolingual dictionaries of languages with generally phonemic orthographies generally don't bother with indicating the pronunciation of most words, and tend to use respelling systems for words with unexpected pronunciations. Dictionaries produced in Israel use the IPA rarely and sometimes use the Hebrew alphabet for transcription of foreign words. Monolingual Hebrew dictionaries use pronunciation respelling for words with unusual spelling; for example, Even-Shoshan Dictionary respells תִּינֹקָה as תִּינְבוֹת because this word uses kamatz katan. Bilingual dictionaries that translate from foreign languages into Russian usually employ the IPA, but monolingual Russian dictionaries occasionally use pronunciation respelling for foreign words; for example, Ozhegov's dictionary adds нэ́ in brackets for the French word пенсне (Pince-nez) to indicate that the e doesn't iotate the н.

The IPA is more common in bilingual dictionaries, but there are exceptions here too. Mass-market bilingual Czech dictionaries, for instance, tend to use the IPA only for sounds not found in the Czech language.[27]

Standard orthographies and capital variants

IPA symbols have been incorporated into the standard orthographies of various languages, notably in Sub-Saharan Africa but in other regions as well, for example: Hausa, Fula, Akan, Gbe languages, Manding languages, and Lingala.

An example of capital letter forms for IPA symbols is Kabiyé of northern Togo, which has Ɔ Ɛ Ɖ Ŋ Ɣ Ʃ Ʊ (or ʊ) (capital ɔ ɛ ɖ ŋ ɣ ʃ ʊ (or ʋ)): *MBƱ AJƐYA KIGBƐNDƱ̃Ʊŋ̃ ŊGBƐYƐ KEDIƔZAƔ SƆSƆƆ TƆM SE.* Other IPA-paired capitals include Ɓ ƇƊ Ǝⱻ Ǥ Ħ Ɯ Ɲ Ɵ Ʈ Ʒ.

The above-mentioned and other capital forms are supported by Unicode, but appear in Latin ranges other than the IPA extensions.

Classical singing

IPA has widespread use among classical singers for preparation, especially among English-speaking singers who rarely sing in their native language. Opera librettos are authoritatively transcribed in IPA, such as Nico Castel's volumes[28] and Timothy Cheek's book *Singing in Czech.*[29] Opera singers' ability to read IPA was recently used by the Visual Thesaurus, which employed several opera singers "to make recordings for the 150,000 words and phrases in VT's lexical database. ...for their vocal stamina, attention to the details of enunciation, and most of all, knowledge of IPA."[30]

Letters

The International Phonetic Alphabet divides its letter symbols into three categories: pulmonic consonants, non-pulmonic consonants, and vowels.[31] [32] Each character is assigned a number, to prevent confusion between similar letters (such as ɵ and θ), for example in printing manuscripts. Different categories of sounds are assigned different ranges of numbers.

Consonants

IPA Pulmonic consonants chart

Place →	Labial		Coronal					Dorsal			Radical		Glottal
↓ Manner	Bila bial	Labio dental	Den tal	Alve olar	Post alv.	Retro flex	Pal a tal	Ve lar	Uvu lar	Pha ryn geal	Epi glot tal	Glot tal
Nasal	m	ɱ	ṇ	n		ɳ	ɲ	ŋ	N			
Plosive	p b	p̪ ḅ	ƚ ɖ	t d		ʈ ɖ	c ɟ	k ɡ	q ɢ		ʔ	ʔ
Fricative	ɸ β	f v	θ ð	s z	ʃ ʒ	ʂ ʐ	ç ʝ	x ɣ	χ ʁ	ħ ʕ	ʜ ʢ	h ɦ
Approximant			ʋ		ɹ		ɻ j		ɰ			
Trill	ʙ			r		• *			R	я *		
Flap or tap	ⱱ			ɾ		ɽ			ɢ̆	ʡ̆		
Lateral Fric.			ɬ ɮ		ɭ̊˔	ʎ̥˔	ʟ̝̊					
Lateral Appr.			l		ɭ	ʎ	L					
Lateral flap			ɺ		ɺ̢ *	ʎ̯						

Non-pulmonic consonants

Clicks	ʘ	ǀ	ǃ	ǂ	ǁ
Implosives	ɓ	ɗ	ʄ	ɠ	ʛ
	pʼ	tʼ	kʼ	qʼ	sʼ
Ejectives	tɬʼ	tʃʼ			

Affricates

pf ts dz tʃ dʒ tɕ dʑ ʈʂ ɖʐ

tɬ dɮ cç ɟʝ

Co-articulated consonants

Fricatives	ɕ	ʑ	ɧ
Approximants	ʍ	w	ɥ ɫ
Stops	k͡p	ɡ͡b	ŋ͡m

These tables contain phonetic symbols, which may not display correctly in some browsers. [Help]

Where symbols appear in pairs, left—right represent the voiceless—voiced consonants.

Shaded areas denote pulmonic articulations judged to be impossible.

* Symbol not defined in IPA.

Pulmonic consonants

A pulmonic consonant is a consonant made by obstructing the glottis (the space between the vocal cords) or oral cavity (the mouth) and either simultaneously or subsequently letting out air from the lungs. Pulmonic consonants make up the majority of consonants in the IPA, as well as in human language. All consonants in the English language fall into this category.[33]

The pulmonic consonant table, which includes most consonants, is arranged in rows that designate manner of articulation, meaning how the consonant is produced, and columns that designate place of articulation, meaning where in the vocal tract the consonant is produced. The main chart includes only consonants with a single place of articulation.

Notes

- Asterisks (*) next to symbols mark reported sounds that do not (yet) have official IPA symbols. See the respective articles for *ad hoc* symbols found in the literature.
- In rows where some symbols appear in pairs (the *obstruents*), the symbol to the right represents a voiced consonant (except breathy-voiced [ɦ]). However, [ʔ] cannot be voiced, and the voicing of [ʔ] is ambiguous.[34] In the other rows (the *sonorants*), the single symbol represents a voiced consonant.
- Although there is a single symbol for the coronal places of articulation for all consonants but fricatives, when dealing with a particular language, the symbols may be treated as specifically dental, alveolar, or post-alveolar, as appropriate for that language, without diacritics.
- Shaded areas indicate articulations judged to be impossible.
- The symbols [ʙ, ʕ, ʢ] represent either voiced fricatives or approximants.
- In many languages, such as English, [h] and [ɦ] are not actually glottal, fricatives, or approximants. Rather, they are bare phonation.[35]
- It is primarily the shape of the tongue rather than its position that distinguishes the fricatives [ʃ ʒ], [ɕ ʑ], and [ʂ ʐ].

Co-articulated consonants

Co-articulated consonants are sounds that involve two simultaneous places of articulation (are pronounced using two parts of the vocal tract). In English, the [w] in "went" is a coarticulated consonant, because it is pronounced by rounding the lips and raising the back of the tongue. Other languages, such as French and Swedish, have different coarticulated consonants.

Note

- [ɧ] is described as a "simultaneous [ʃ] and [x]".[36] However, this analysis is disputed. (See voiceless palatal-velar fricative for discussion.)

Affricates and double articulated consonants

Affricates and doubly articulated stops are represented by two symbols joined by a tie bar, either above or below the symbols. The six most common affricates are optionally represented by ligatures, though this is no longer official IPA usage,[1] because a great number of ligatures would be required to represent all affricates this way. Alternatively, a superscript notation for a consonant release is sometimes used to transcribe affricates, for example t^s for t͡s, paralleling k^x ~ k͡x. The symbols for the palatal plosives c and ɟ, are often used as a convenience for t͡ʃ and d͡ʒ or similar affricates, even in official IPA publications, so they must be interpreted with care.

View this table as an image.		
Tie bar	**Ligature**	**Description**
t͡s	ʦ	voiceless alveolar affricate
d͡z	ʣ	voiced alveolar affricate
t͡ʃ	ʧ	voiceless postalveolar affricate
d͡ʒ	ʤ	voiced postalveolar affricate
t͡ɕ	ʨ	voiceless alveolo-palatal affricate
d͡ʑ	ʥ	voiced alveolo-palatal affricate
t͡ɬ	–	voiceless alveolar lateral affricate
k͡p	–	voiceless labial-velar plosive
g͡b	–	voiced labial-velar plosive
ŋ͡m	–	labial-velar nasal stop

Note

- On browsers that use *Arial Unicode MS* to display IPA characters, the following incorrectly formed sequences may look better due to a bug in that font: t͡s, t͡ʃ, t͡ɕ, d͡z, d͡ʒ, d͡ʑ, t͡ɬ, k͡p, g͡b, ŋ͡m.

Non-pulmonic consonants

Non-pulmonic consonants are sounds whose airflow is not dependent on the lungs. These include clicks (found in the Khoisan languages of Africa), implosives (found in languages such as Swahili) and ejectives (found in many Amerindian and Caucasian languages).

View this table as an image					
Clicks		**Implosives**		**Ejectives**	
ʘ	Bilabial	ɓ	Bilabial	'	*For example:*
ǀ	Laminal alveolar ("dental")	ɗ	Alveolar	p'	Bilabial
ǃ	Apical (post-) alveolar ("retroflex")	ʄ	Palatal	t'	Alveolar
ǂ	Laminal postalveolar ("palatal")	ɠ	Velar	k'	Velar
ǁ	Lateral coronal ("lateral")	ʛ	Uvular	s'	Alveolar fricative

Notes

- Clicks are double articulated and have traditionally been described as having a forward 'release' and a rear 'accompaniment', with the click letters representing the release. Therefore all clicks would require two letters for proper notation: ⟨k͜ǂ, g͜ǂ, ŋ͜ǂ, q͜ǂ, ɢ͜ǂ, ɴ͜ǂ⟩ *etc.*, or ⟨ǂ͜k, ǂ͜g, ǂ͜ŋ, ǂ͜q, ǂ͜ɢ, ǂ͜ɴ⟩. When the dorsal articulation is omitted, a [k] may usually be assumed. However, recent research disputes the concept of 'accompaniment'.[37] In these approaches, the click letter represents both articulations, there is no velar-uvular distinction, and the accompanying letter represents the manner of the click: ‹ǂ, ᶢǂ, ᵑǂ› etc.

- Symbols for the voiceless implosives ‹ƥ, ƭ, ƈ, ƙ, ʠ› are no longer supported by the IPA, though they remain in Unicode. Instead, the IPA typically uses the voiced equivalent with a voiceless diacritic: ‹ɓ̥, ʛ̥, etc.
- Although not confirmed as contrastive in any language, and therefore not explicitly recognized by the IPA, a letter for the retroflex implosive, ‹ ›, is supported in the Unicode Phonetic Extensions Supplement, added in version 4.1 of the Unicode Standard, or can be created as a composite ‹ɖ̓›.
- The ejective symbol often stands in for a superscript glottal stop in glottalized but pulmonic sonorants, such as [mˀ], [lˀ], [wˀ], [aˀ]. These may also be transcribed as creaky [m̰], [l̰], [w̰], [a̰].

Vowels

IPA vowel chart (Chart image)

	Front	Near-front	Central	Near-back	Back
Close					
Near-close					
Close-mid			i · y		
			ɨ · ʉ		
			ɯ · u		
Mid			ɪ · ʏ		
			ɪ̈ · ʊ̈		
			· ʊ		
			e · ø		
Open-mid			ə̝ · ɘ		
			ɤ̞ · o		
			ə		
Near-open			ɛ · œ		
			ɜ · ɞ		
			ʌ · ɔ		
			æ ·		
Open			ɐ		
			a · ɶ		
			ɑ · ɒ		

Left and right of a bullet are unrounded · rounded vowels

The IPA defines a vowel as a sound which occurs at a syllable center.[38] Below is a chart depicting the vowels of the IPA. The IPA maps the vowels according to the position of the tongue.

The vertical axis of the chart is mapped by vowel height. Vowels pronounced with the tongue lowered are at the bottom, and vowels pronounced with the tongue raised are at the top. For example, [ɑ] (said as the "a" in "palm") is at the bottom because the tongue is lowered in this position. However, [i] (said as the vowel in "meet") is at the top because the sound is said with the tongue raised to the roof of the mouth.

In a similar fashion, the horizontal axis of the chart is determined by vowel backness. Vowels with the tongue moved towards the front of the mouth (such as [ɛ], the vowel in "met") are to the left in the chart, while those in which it is moved to the back (such as [ʌ], the vowel in "but") are placed to the right in the chart.

In places where vowels are paired, the right represents a rounded vowel (in which the lips are rounded) while the left is its unrounded counterpart.

Notes

* ⟨a⟩ officially represents a front vowel, but there is little distinction between front and central open vowels, and ⟨a⟩ is frequently used for an open central vowel.[19] However, if disambiguation is required, the retraction diacritic or the centralized diacritic may be added to indicate an open central vowel, as in ⟨a̠⟩ or ⟨ä⟩.

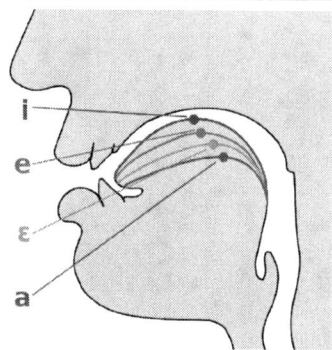

Tongue positions of cardinal front vowels with highest point indicated. The position of the highest point is used to determine vowel height and backness

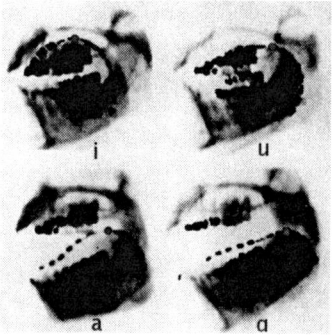

An X-ray film shows the sounds [i, u, a, ɑ]

Diacritics

Diacritics are small markings which are placed around the IPA letter in order to show a certain alteration or more specific description in the letter's pronunciation.[39] Sub-diacritics (markings normally placed below a letter or symbol) may be placed above a symbol having a descender (informally called a tail), e.g. ɳ̊, j̊.[39]

The dotless *i*, ⟨ı⟩, is used when the dot would interfere with the diacritic. Other IPA symbols may appear as diacritics to represent phonetic detail: tˢ (fricative release), bʰ (breathy voice), ʔa (glottal onset), (epenthetic schwa), oᵁ (diphthongization). Additional diacritics were introduced in the Extensions to the IPA, which were designed principally for speech pathology.

View the diacritic table as an image					
Syllabicity diacritics					
	ɹ̩ ŋ̍	Syllabic		e̯ ʊ̯	Non-syllabic
Consonant-release diacritics					
h	tʰ	Aspirated[a]	˺	d̚	No audible release
ɦ	dʰ				
n	dⁿ	Nasal release	l	dˡ	Lateral release
Phonation diacritics					
̥	n̥ d̥	Voiceless		s̬ t̬	Voiced
̤	b̤ a̤	Breathy voiced[b]		b̰ a̰	Creaky voiced
Articulation diacritics					
̪	t̪ d̪	Dental		t̼ d̼	Linguolabial
̺	t̺ d̺	Apical		t̻ d̻	Laminal
̟	u̟ t̟	Advanced		i̠ t̠	Retracted
̈	ë ä	Centralized	×	ė ẅ	Mid-centralized
̝ ˔	e̝ ɹ̝	Raised (ɹ̝ = voiced alveolar nonsibilant fricative)			
̞ ˕	e̞ β̞	Lowered (β̞ = bilabial approximant)			
Co-articulation diacritics					
̹	ɔ̹ x̹	More rounded		ɔ̜ x̜ʷ	Less rounded
w	tʷ dʷ	Labialized or labio-velarized	j	tʲ dʲ	Palatalized
ɣ	tˠ dˠ	Velarized	ˤ	tˤ aˤ	Pharyngealized
ɥ	tᶣ dᶣ	Labio-palatalized	̴	ɫ z̴	Velarized *or* pharyngealized
̘	e̘ o̘	Advanced tongue root		e̙ o̙	Retracted tongue root
̃	ẽ z̃	Nasalized		ɚ ɝ	Rhotacized

Notes

   a With aspirated voiced consonants, the aspiration is also voiced. Many linguists prefer one of the diacritics dedicated to breathy voice.

   b Some linguists restrict this breathy-voice diacritic to sonorants, and transcribe obstruents as bʰ.

The state of the glottis can be finely transcribed with diacritics. A series of alveolar plosives ranging from an open to a closed glottis phonation are:

[t]	voiceless	••	[d̤]	breathy voice, also called *murmured*	
[d̠]	slack voice	̥	[d]	modal voice	
[d̟]	stiff voice	̰	[d̰]	creaky voice	
ʔ [ʔ͡t]	glottal closure				

Suprasegmentals

These symbols describe the features of a language above the level of individual consonants and vowels, such as prosody, tone, length, and stress, which often operate on syllables, words, or phrases: that is, elements such as the intensity, pitch, and gemination of the sounds of a language, as well as the rhythm and intonation of speech.[40] Although most of these symbols indicate distinctions that are phonemic at the word level, symbols also exist for intonation on a level greater than that of the word.[40]

View this table as an image			
Length, stress, and rhythm			
ˈa	Primary stress (symbol goes before stressed syllable)	ˌa	Secondary stress (symbol goes before stressed syllable)
aː kː	Long (long vowel or geminate consonant)	aˑ	Half-long
ă	Extra-short	a.a	Syllable break
s‿a	Linking (absence of a break)		
Intonation			
ǀ	Minor (foot) break	‖	Major (intonation) break
↗	Global rise	↘	Global fall
Tone diacritics and tone letters			
ŋ̋ e̋ e˥	Extra high / top	ꜛe	Upstep
ŋ́ é e˦	High	ŋ̌ ě	Rise
ŋ̄ ē e˧	Mid		
ŋ̀ è e˨	Low	ŋ̂ ê	Fall
ŋ̏ ȅ e˩	Extra low / bottom	ꜜe	Downstep

Finer distinctions of tone may be indicated by combining the tone diacritics and letters shown here, though not many fonts support this. The primary examples are high (mid) rising ɔ, ɔ˦˥; low rising ɔ, ɔ˩˦; high falling ɔ, ɔ˥˦; low (mid) falling ɔ, ɔ˦˩; peaking ɔ, ɔ˦˥˦; and dipping ɔ, ɔ˦˩˦. A work-around for diacritics sometimes seen when a language has more than one rising or falling tone, and the author does not wish to completely abandon the IPA, is to restrict generic rising ɔ̌ and falling ɔ̂ for the higher-pitched of the rising and falling tones, ɔ˥˦ and ɔ˦˥, and to use the non-standard subscript diacritics ◌ and ◌ for the lower-pitched rising and falling tones, ɔ˩˦ and ɔ˦˩. When a language has four level tones, the two mid tones are sometimes transcribed as high-mid ɔ́ (non-standard) and low-mid ɔ̄.

Obsolete symbols and nonstandard symbols

The IPA inherited alternate symbols from various traditions, but eventually settled on one for each sound. The other symbols are now considered obsolete. An example is ‹ɷ› which has been standardised to ‹ʊ›. Several symbols indicating secondary articulation have been dropped altogether, with the idea that such things should be indicated with diacritics: ‹ƍ› for ‹zʷ› is one. In addition, the rare voiceless implosive series ‹ƥ ƭ ƈ ƙ ʠ› has been dropped; they are now written ‹ɓ̥ ɗ̥ ʄ̥ ɠ̥ ɢ̥› or ‹p'↓ t'↓ c'↓ k'↓ q'↓› respectively. A rejected competing proposal for transcribing clicks, ʇ, ɔ, ʖ, is still sometimes seen, as the official letters ǀ, ǃ, ǁ may cause problems with legibility, especially when used with brackets, the letter ǀ, or the prosodic marks ǀ, ǁ.[41]

There are also unsupported or *ad hoc* symbols from local traditions that find their way into publications that otherwise use the standard IPA. This is especially common with affricates such as the "barred lambda" ‹ƛ› for [tɬ].

IPA extensions

Extensions to the IPA, also often abbreviated as extIPA, is a group of symbols whose original purpose was to accurately transcribe disordered speech. At the IPA Kiel Convention in 1989, a group of linguists drew up the initial set of symbols for the Extended IPA.[42] Extensions to the IPA were first published in 1990, and modified over the next few years before its official publication in the *Journal of the International Phonetic Association* in 1994 allowed it to be officially adopted by the ICPLA.[43] While its original purpose was to transcribe disordered speech, linguists have used it to designate a number of unique sounds within standard communication, such as hushing, gnashing teeth, and smacking lips. The Extensions to the IPA have also been used to record certain peculiarities in an individual's voice, such as nasalized voicing.[3]

Aside from the extIPA, another set of symbols is used for voice quality (VoQS), such as whispering.

Segments that have no symbols

The remaining blank cells on the IPA chart can be filled without too much difficulty if the need arises. Some *ad hoc* symbols have appeared in the literature, for example for the retroflex lateral flap and the voiceless lateral fricative series, the epiglottal trill, and the labiodental plosives. (See the grey symbols in the PDF chart.) Diacritics can supply much of the remainder, which would indeed be appropriate if the sounds were allophones.[44]

Consonants without letters

Representations of consonant sounds outside of the core set are created by adding diacritics to symbols for similar sound values. The Spanish bilabial and dental approximants are commonly written as lowered fricatives, [β̞] and [ð̞] respectively. Similarly, voiced lateral fricatives would be written as raised lateral approximants, [ɭ̝ ʎ̝ ʟ̝]. A few languages such as Banda have a bilabial flap as the preferred allophone of what is elsewhere a labiodental flap. It has been suggested that this be written with the labiodental flap symbol and the advanced diacritic, [ⱱ̟].[45]

Similarly, a labiodental trill would be written [ʙ̪] (bilabial trill and the dental sign), and labiodental stops [p̪ b̪] rather than with the *ad hoc* symbols sometimes found in the literature. Other taps can be written as extra-short plosives or laterals, e.g. [ɟ̆ ɢ̆/ʀ̆ ɺ̆], though in some cases the diacritic would need to be written below the letter. A retroflex trill can be written as a retracted [r̠], just as retroflex fricatives sometimes are. The remaining consonants, the uvular laterals (ʟ̠ etc.) and the palatal trill, while not strictly impossible, are very difficult to pronounce and are unlikely to occur even as allophones in the world's languages.

Vowels without letters

The vowels are similarly manageable by using diacritics for raising, lowering, fronting, backing, centering, and mid-centering.[46] For example, the unrounded equivalent of [ʊ] can be transcribed as mid-centered [ɯ̽], and the rounded equivalent of [æ] as raised [æ̝]. True mid vowels are lowered [e̞ ø̞ ɘ̞ ɵ̞ ɤ̞ o̞], while centered [ɪ̈ ʊ̈] and [ä] are near-close and open central vowels, respectively. The only known vowels that cannot be represented in this scheme are vowels with unexpected roundedness, which would require a dedicated diacritic, such as [ɤ̜] or [ɯ̹].

Symbol names

An IPA symbol is often distinguished from the sound it is intended to represent since there is not a one-to-one correspondence between symbol and sound in broad transcription. While the *Handbook of the International Phonetic Association* states that no official names exist for symbols, it admits the presence of one or two common names for each character that are commonly used.[47] The symbols also have nonce names in the Unicode standard. In some cases, the Unicode names and the IPA do not agree. For example, IPA calls ε "epsilon", but Unicode calls it "small letter open E".

The traditional names of the Latin and Greek letters are usually used for unmodified symbols.[48] Letters which are not directly derived from these alphabets, such as [ʕ], may have a variety of names, sometimes based on the appearance of the symbol, and sometimes based on the sound that it represents. In Unicode, some of the symbols of Greek origin have Latin forms for use in IPA; the others use the symbols from the Greek section.

For diacritics, there are two methods of naming. For traditional diacritics, the IPA uses the name of the symbol from a certain language, for example, é is *acute*, based on the name of the symbol in English and French. In non-traditional diacritics, the IPA often names a symbol according to an object it resembles, as ḓ is called *bridge*.

ASCII and keyboard transliterations

Several systems have been developed that map the IPA symbols to ASCII characters. Notable systems include Kirshenbaum, SAMPA, and X-SAMPA. The usage of mapping systems in on-line text has to some extent been adopted in the context input methods, allowing convenient keying of IPA characters that would be otherwise unavailable on standard keyboard layouts.

See also

- Articulatory phonetics
- Index of phonetics articles
- International Alphabet of Sanskrit Transliteration
- IPA chart for English dialects
- List of international common standards
- Luciano Canepari
- Phonetic transcription
- Semyon Novgorodov - inventor of IPA-based Yakut alphabet
- TIPA provides IPA support for LaTeX
- Unicode Phonetic Symbols
- ICAO spelling alphabet
- Wikipedia:IPA for English

Further reading

- Ball, Martin J.; John H. Esling & B. Craig. Dickson (1995). "The VoQS system for the transcription of voice quality". *Journal of the International Phonetic Alphabet* **25** (2): 71–80. doi:10.1017/S0025100300005181.
- Duckworth, M.; G. Allen, M.J. Ball (December 1990). "Extensions to the International Phonetic Alphabet for the transcription of atypical speech". *Clinical Linguistics and Phonetics* **4** (4): 273–280.
- Hill, Kenneth C. (March 1988). "Review of *Phonetic symbol guide* by G. K. Pullum & W. Ladusaw". *Language* **64** (1): 143–144. doi:10.2307/414792.
- International Phonetic Association (1989). "Report on the 1989 Kiel convention". *Journal of the International Phonetic Alphabet* **19** (2): 67–80.
- International Phonetic Association (1999). *Handbook of the International Phonetic Association: A guide to the use of the International Phonetic Alphabet.* Cambridge: Cambridge University Press. ISBN 0-521-65236-7 (hb); ISBN 0-521-63751-1 (pb).
- Jones, Daniel (1988). *English pronouncing dictionary* (revised 14th ed.). London: Dent. OCLC 18415701.
- Ladefoged, Peter (September 1990). "The revised International Phonetic Alphabet". *Language* **66** (3): 550–552. doi:10.2307/414611.
- Ladefoged, Peter; Morris Hale (September 1988). "Some major features of the International Phonetic Alphabet". *Language* **64** (3): 577–582. doi:10.2307/414533.
- Laver, John (1994). *Principles of Phonetics.* New York: Cambridge University Press. ISBN 0-521-45031-4 (hb); ISBN 0-521-45655-X (pb).
- Pullum, Geoffrey K.; William A. Laduslaw (1986). *Phonetic symbol guide.* Chicago: University of Chicago Press. ISBN 0-226-68532-2.
- Skinner, Edith; Timothy Monich, and Lilene Mansell (1990). *Speak with Distinction.* New York, NY: Applause Theatre Book Publishers.

External links

- Video recordings of the sounds of IPA by The University of Sheffield [49]
- Information on IPA by Omniglot [50]
- IPA Chart [51] in Unicode and XHTML/CSS
- IPA copy & paste charts, keyboards, etc by IPA.Webstuff.org [52]
- Learning the IPA for English [53], (Standard American English)
- The International Phonetic Association web site [54]
- Various resources including a glossary [55] by Peter Roach, Professor of Phonetics, University of Cambridge, UK
- The International Phonetic Alphabet (revised to 2005) [56] Symbols for all languages are shown on this one-page chart
- Using IPA fonts with Mac OS X: The Comprehensive Guide [57], an article explaining how to install and use freeware fonts and keyboard layouts to type in the International Phonetic Alphabet on OS X
- Visual Thesaurus [58]
- IPA - Introduction [59] This site was especially designed to act as an introduction to the English Phonetic Alphabet. All of the sounds and symbols within the IPA that are associated with the English language are included. IPA symbols are displayed in square brackets ([]). Please browse this site to find out more about the International Phonetic Alphabet.

Education

- Interactive Saggital Section [60]
- Phonetics: the Sounds of English and Spanish [61] Note: requires Flash 7 or higher.
- IPA Charts with an interactive chart of all IPA symbols with their sounds (Flash) [62]

IPA font downloads

- Charis SIL [63], a very complete international font (Latin, Greek, Cyrillic) in roman, italic, and bold typefaces that includes tone letters and pre-composed tone diacritics on IPA vowels, the new labiodental flap, and many non-standard phonetic symbols. Based on Bitstream Charter, this font suffers from extremely bad hinting when rendered by FreeType on Linux.
- DejaVu fonts Sourceforge.net [64] have full Unicode IPA support. Sourceforge.net [65]
- Doulos SIL [66], a Times/Times New Roman style font. It contains the same characters as Charis SIL, but only in a single face, roman.
- Gentium [67], a professionally designed international font (Latin, Greek, Cyrillic) in roman and italic typefaces that includes the IPA, but not yet tone letters or the new labiodental flap. For bold typefaces but only the most basic IPA letters, Gentium Basic may be used.
- TIPA [68], a font and system for entering IPA phonetic transcriptions in LaTeX documents.

Keyboard input

- Complete Guide [69]: Beginners' guide to using IPA on Windows, Mac OS and Linux, covering many office applications and browsers
- Downloadable IPA keyboard layout for Microsoft Windows [70] for Unicode IPA input
- Downloadable IPA-SIL keyboard layout for Mac OS X [71] for Unicode IPA input
- IPA Character Picker [72] Web-based input method
- IPA Palette [73] is the Mac OS X version of IPACharMap.
- IPACharMap (scroll down to see it) [74] is an on-screen keyboard for point and click character entry, which can then be copied and pasted into a unicode-aware word processor. Based on IPA Palette.
- IPATotal keyboard [75] - This free UNICODE based keyboard encodes the whole character and diacritics charts of the International Phonetic Alphabet (IPA), designed to represent all the sounds of speech in any language.
- IPA Writer [76]: The IPA Writer. Online tool to write IPA.
- Microsoft Template [77] - Creates a Toolbar for Microsoft Word. (This uses macros)
- Online keyboard [78]
- Online keyboard [79] with MP3 sound files for IPA symbols
- IPAEdit [80] Unicode-compliant Transcription Editor for Linux, Mac OS X and Windows from the University of Marburg
- PhonPad [81] online IPA editor.

Sound files

- An introduction to the sounds of languages [82]
- Complete IPA chart with sound samples, including English diphthongs [62]
- IPA chart [83] with MP3 sound files for all IPA symbols on the chart (limited version is available to anyone)
- IPA chart [84] with AIFF sound files for IPA symbols
- Peter Ladefoged's Course in Phonetics (with sound files) [85]

Unicode charts

- International Phonetic Alphabet in Unicode [86]
- Unicode chart for main IPA letters [87]PDF (246.8 KB)
- Unicode chart for IPA modifier letters [88]PDF (203 KB)
- Unicode chart including IPA diacritics [89]PDF (231.2 KB)
- IPA with Unicode superimposed [90]PDF (1.6 MB) from the University of Marburg
- MySQL Unicode collation chart for IPA and other phonetic blocks [91]
- Unicode-HTML codes for IPA symbols: [92] Tables of symbol names, character entity references and/or numeric character references at PennState.

References

[1] "The acronym 'IPA' strictly refers [...] to the 'International Phonetic Association'. But it is now such a common practice to use the acronym also to refer to the alphabet itself (from the phrase 'International Phonetic Alphabet') that resistance seems pedantic. Context usually serves to disambiguate the two usages." (Laver 1994:561)

[2] International Phonetic Association (IPA), Handbook.

[3] MacMahon, Michael K. C. (1996). "Phonetic Notation". in P. T. Daniels and W. Bright (eds.). The World's Writing Systems. New York: Oxford University Press. pp. 821–846. ISBN 0-19-507993-0.

[4] Wall, Joan (1989). International Phonetic Alphabet for Singers: A Manual for English and Foreign Language Diction (http://www.amazon.com/International-Phonetic-Alphabet-Singers-Language/dp/1877761508). Pst. ISBN 1877761508. .

[5] International Phonetic Association, Handbook, pp. 194–196

[6] "Originally, the aim was to make available a set of phonetic symbols which would be given different articulatory values, if necessary, in different languages." (International Phonetic Association, Handbook, pp. 195–196)

[7] Passy, Paul (1888). "Our revised alphabet". The Phonetic Teacher: 57–60.

[8] Pullum and Ladusaw, Phonetic Symbol Guide, pp. 152, 209

[9] Nicolaidis, Katerina (September 2005). "Approval of New IPA Sound: The Labiodental Flap" (http://www2.arts.gla.ac.uk/IPA/flap.htm). International Phonetic Association. . Retrieved 2006-09-17.

[10] International Phonetic Association, Handbook, p. 186

[11] "From its earliest days...the International Phonetic Association has aimed to provide 'a separate sign for each distinctive sound; that is, for each sound which, being used instead of another, in the same language, can change the meaning of a word'." (International Phonetic Association, Handbook, p. 27)

[12] In contrast, English sometimes uses combinations of two letters to represent single sounds, such as the digraphs sh and th for the sounds [ʃ] and [θ]~[ð], respectively.

[13] For instance, flaps and taps are two different kinds of articulation, but since no language has (yet) been found to make a distinction between, say, an alveolar flap and an alveolar tap, the IPA does not provide such sounds with dedicated symbols. Instead, it provides a single symbol (in this case, [ɾ]) for both sounds. Strictly speaking, this makes the IPA a phonemic alphabet, not a phonetic one.

[14] There are five basic tone marks, which are combined for contour tones; six of these combinations are in common use.

[15] "The non-roman letters of the International Phonetic Alphabet have been designed as far as possible to harmonize well with the roman letters. The Association does not recognise makeshift letters; It recognises only letters which have been carefully cut so as to be in harmony with the other letters." (IPA 1949)

[16] Technically, the symbol [ʔ] could be considered Latin-derived, since the question mark may have originated as "Qo", an abbreviation of the Latin word quæstio, "question".

[17] Laver, Principles of Phonetics, pp. 174–175

[18] "The new letters should be suggestive of the sounds they represent, by their resemblance to the old ones." (International Phonetic Association, Handbook, p. 196)

[19] Sally Thomason (January 2, 2008). "Why I Don't Love the International Phonetic Alphabet" (http://itre.cis.upenn.edu/~myl/languagelog/archives/005287.html). Language Log. .

[20] For example, the English school textbooks by I.N.Vereshagina, K.A. Bondarenko and T.A. Pritykina.

[21] For example, "Le Français à la portée de tous" by K.K. Parchevsky and E.B. Roisenblit (1995) and "English Through Eye and Ear" by L.V. Bankevich (1975).

[22] "Phonetics" (http://dictionary.cambridge.org/help/phonetics.htm). Cambridge Dictionaries Online. 2002. . Retrieved 2007-03-11.

[23] "Merriam-Webster Online Pronunciation Symbols" (http://mw1.merriam-webster.com/pronsymbols.html). . Retrieved 2007-06-04. Agnes, Michael (1999). Webster's New World College Dictionary. New York, NY: Macmillan USA. xxiii. ISBN 0-02-863119-6. Pronunciation respelling for English has detailed comparisons.

[24] http://www.bartleby.com/61/46/C0674600.html

[25] http://www.bartleby.com/61/14/C0171400.html

[26] "Pronunciation Key" (http://www.bartleby.com/61/12.html). The American Heritage Dictionary of the English Language. Bartleby.com. 2000. . Retrieved 2006-09-19.

[27] (Czech) Fronek, J. (2006) (in Czech). Velký anglicko-český slovník. Praha: Leda. ISBN 80-7335-022-X. "In accordance with long-established Czech lexicographical tradition, a modified version of the International Phonetic Alphabet (IPA) is adopted in which letters of the Czech alphabet are employed."

[28] "Nico Castel's Complete Libretti Series" (http://www.castelopera.com/libretti.htm). Castel Opera Arts. . Retrieved 2008-09-29.

[29] Cheek, Timothy (2001). Singing in Czech (http://scarecrowpress.com/Catalog/SingleBook.shtml?command=Search&db=^DB/ CATALOG.db&eqSKUdata=0810840030). The Scarecrow Press. pp. 392. ISBN 0-8108-4003-0 ISBN 978-0-8108-4003-4. .

[30] Zimmer, Benjamin (2008-05-14). "Operatic IPA and the Visual Thesaurus" (http://languagelog.ldc.upenn.edu/nll/?p=155). Language Log. University of Pennsylvania. . Retrieved 2009-09-29.

[31] "Segments can usefully be divided into two major categories, consonants and vowels." (International Phonetic Association, Handbook, p. 3)

[32] International Phonetic Association, Handbook, p. 6.

[33] Fromkin, Victoria; Rodman, Robert (1998) [1974]. An Introduction to Language (6th ed.). Fort Worth, TX: Harcourt Brace College Publishers. ISBN 0-03-018682-X.

[34] Ladefoged and Maddieson, 1996, Sounds of the World's Languages, §2.1.

[35] Ladefoged and Maddieson, 1996, Sounds of the World's Languages, §9.3.

[36] Ladefoged, Peter; Ian Maddieson (1996). The sounds of the world's languages. Oxford: Blackwell. pp. 329–330. ISBN 0-631-19815-6.

[37] Amanda L. Miller et al., "Differences in airstream and posterior place of articulation among Nluu lingual stops" (http://ling.cornell.edu/ plab/amanda/amiller_jipa.pdf). Submitted to the Journal of the International Phonetic Association. Retrieved 2007-05-27.

[38] International Phonetic Association, Handbook, p. 10.

[39] International Phonetic Association, Handbook, pp. 14–15.

[40] International Phonetic Association, Handbook, p. 13.

[41] John Wells's phonetic blog (http://phonetic-blog.blogspot.com/2009/09/click-symbols.html)

[42] "At the 1989 Kiel Convention of the IPA, a sub-group was established to draw up recommendations for the transcription of disordered speech." ("Extensions to the IPA: An ExtIPA Chart" in International Phonetic Association, Handbook, pp. 186.)

[43] "Extensions to the IPA: An ExtIPA Chart" in International Phonetic Association, Handbook, pp. 186–187.

[44] "Diacritics may also be employed to create symbols for phonemes, thus reducing the need to create new letter shapes." (International Phonetic Association, Handbook, p. 27)

[45] Olson, Kenneth S.; & Hajek, John. (1999). The phonetic status of the labial flap. Journal of the International Phonetic Association, 29 (2), pp. 101–114.

[46] "The diacrtics...can be used to modify the lip or tongue position implied by a vowel symbol." (International Phonetic Association, Handbook, p. 16)

[47] "...the International Phonetic Association has never officially approved a set of names..." (International Phonetic Association, Handbook, p. 31)

[48] For example, [p] is called "Lower-case P" and [χ] is "Chi." (International Phonetic Association, Handbook, p. 171)

[49] http://www.shef.ac.uk/ipa/index.php

[50] http://www.omniglot.com/writing/ipa.htm

[51] http://weston.ruter.net/projects/ipa-chart/view/

[52] http://www.ipa.webstuff.org/

[53] http://cla.calpoly.edu/~jrubba/phon/learnipa.html

[54] http://www.langsci.ucl.ac.uk/ipa/

[55] http://www.cambridge.org/elt/peterroach/resources.htm

[56] http://www.langsci.ucl.ac.uk/ipa/IPA_chart_(C)2005.pdf

[57] http://linguisticmystic.com/2007/03/08/using-ipa-fonts-with-mac-os-x-the-comprehensive-guide/

[58] http://www.visualthesaurus.com/howitworks/

[59] http://web.ku.edu/~cmed/ipafolder/index.html

[60] http://www.chass.utoronto.ca/~danhall/phonetics/sammy.html

[61] http://www.uiowa.edu/~acadtech/phonetics/#

[62] http://www.yorku.ca/earmstro/ipa/

[63] http://scripts.sil.org/CharisSILfont

[64] http://dejavu.sourceforge.net/wiki/index.php/Download
[65] http://dejavu.svn.sourceforge.net/viewvc/dejavu/trunk/dejavu-fonts/unicover.txt
[66] http://scripts.sil.org/DoulosSILfont
[67] http://scripts.sil.org/FontDownloadsGentium
[68] http://tug.ctan.org/cgi-bin/ctanPackageInformation.py?id=tipa
[69] http://ipa4linguists.pbwiki.com/
[70] http://www.rejc2.co.uk/ipakeyboard/
[71] http://scripts.sil.org/cms/scripts/page.php?site_id=nrsi&item_id=ipa-sil_keyboard
[72] http://rishida.net/scripts/pickers/ipa/
[73] http://www.blugs.com/IPA/
[74] http://www.davidmontero.net/Linguistics.php
[75] http://keymankeyboards.com/?id=454
[76] http://ipatrainer.com/user/ipawriter/
[77] http://www.jamesabela.co.uk/beginner/IPA.htm
[78] http://www.linguiste.org/phonetics/ipa/chart/keyboard/
[79] http://webmasterei.com/en/tools/ipa
[80] http://www.uni-marburg.de/fb09/dsa/mitarbeiter/lueders/applications
[81] http://www.lfsag.unito.it/ipa/editor_en.html
[82] http://hctv.humnet.ucla.edu/departments/linguistics/VowelsandConsonants/vowels/contents.html
[83] http://web.uvic.ca/ling/resources/ipa/ipa-lab.htm
[84] http://hctv.humnet.ucla.edu/departments/linguistics/VowelsandConsonants/course/chapter1/chapter1.html
[85] http://hctv.humnet.ucla.edu/departments/linguistics/VowelsandConsonants/
[86] http://www.phon.ucl.ac.uk/home/wells/ipa-unicode.htm
[87] http://www.unicode.org/charts/PDF/U0250.pdf
[88] http://www.unicode.org/charts/PDF/U02B0.pdf
[89] http://www.unicode.org/charts/PDF/U0300.pdf
[90] http://www.staff.uni-marburg.de/%7Eluedersb/IPA_CHART2005-UNICODE.pdf
[91] http://www.collation-charts.org/mysql60/mysql604.utf8_unicode_ci.phonetic.html
[92] http://tlt.its.psu.edu/suggestions/international/bylanguage/ipachart.html

Salishan languages

This article is about the Salish/Salishan language. For the Tacoma, Washington, neighborhood, see Salishan, Tacoma, Washington.

Salishan	
Geographic distribution:	Pacific Northwest and Interior Plateau/Columbia Plateau in Canada and the United States
Genetic classification:	
Subdivisions:	Coast Salish Interior Salish Tsamosan *Nuxálk* *Tillamook*
ISO 639-2 and 639-5:	sal

Pre-contact distribution of Salishan languages (in red).

The **Salishan** (also **Salish**) languages are a group of languages of the Pacific Northwest (the Canadian province of British Columbia and the American states of Washington, Oregon, Idaho and Montana).[1] They are characterised by agglutinativity and astonishing consonant clusters — for instance the Nuxálk word *xłp̓x̌ʷłtłpłłskʷc̓* (IPA: [xɬpʼχʷɬtʰɬpʰɬːskʷʰts̓]) meaning "he had had a bunchberry plant" has 13 consonants in a row with no vowels.

The terms *Salish* and *Salishan* are used interchangeably by Salishan linguists and anthropologists. The name *Salish* is actually the endonym of the Flathead Nation. The name was later extended by linguists to refer to other related languages. Many languages do not have self-designations and instead have specific names for local dialects as the local group was more important culturally than larger tribal relations.

All Salishan languages which are not extinct are endangered—some extremely so with only three or four speakers left. Practically all languages only have speakers who are over sixty years of age, and many languages only have speakers over eighty. Salish is most commonly written using the Americanist phonetic notation to account for the various vowels and consonants that do not exist in most modern alphabets.

Family division

The Salishan language family consists of twenty-three languages. Below is a list of Salishan languages, dialects, and sub-dialects. This list is a linguistic classification that may not correspond to political divisions. Many Salishan groups consider their variety of speech to be a separate language rather than a dialect.

Bella Coola

1. **Nuxálk** (a.k.a. Bella Coola, Salmon River)

- Kimsquit
- Bella Coola
- Kwatna
- Tallheo

Coast Salish

A. Central Coast Salish (a.k.a. Central Salish)

Flathead Indians (1903)

2. **Comox**

- Island Comox (a.k.a. Q'ómoxʷs)
- Sliammon (Homalco-Klahoose-Sliammon) (a.k.a. ʔayʔajúθəm)

3. **Halkomelem**

Island (a.k.a. Hul'q'umi'num', həlq̓əmín̓əm̓)

- Cowichan
- Snuneymuxw/Nanaimo

Downriver (a.k.a. Hunq'um?i?num?)

- Musqueam

Upriver (a.k.a. Upper Sto:lo, Halq'əméyləm)

- Katzie
- Kwantlen
- Chehalis (Canada)
- Chilliwack
- Tait
- Skway

4. **Lushootseed** (a.k.a. Puget Salish, Skagit-Nisqually, Dxʷləšúcid)

Northern

- Skagit (a.k.a. Skaǰət)
- Snohomish (a.k.a. Sduhubš)

Southern

- Duwamish-Suquamish (a.k.a. Dxʷduʔabš)
- Puyallup (a.k.a. Spuyaləpubš)
- Nisqually (a.k.a. Sqʷaliʔabš)

5. **Nooksack** (a.k.a. Nooksack łéčələsəm, łéčælosəm) *(†)*

6. **Pentlatch** (a.k.a. Pənƛ̓áč) *(†)*

7. **Sháshíshálh** (a.k.a. Sechelt, Seshelt, Shashishalhem, šášíšátəm)

8. **Squamish** (a.k.a. Sḵwx̱wú7mesh snichim, Sḵwx̱wú7mesh, Sqwxwu7mish, sqʷxʷúʔməš)

i. Straits Salish group (a.k.a. Straits)

9. **Klallam** (a.k.a. Clallam, Nəxʷsx̌áẏemúcən)

- Becher Bay
- Eastern
- Western

10. **Northern Straits** (a.k.a. Straits)

- Lummi (a.k.a. Xwlemi'chosen, xʷləmiʔčósən) *(†)*
- Saanich (a.k.a. SENĆOŦEN, sənčáθən, sénəčqən)
- Samish (a.k.a. Siʔneməš)
- Semiahmoo (a.k.a. Tah-tu-lo) *(†)*
- Sooke (a.k.a. T'sou-ke, ćawk) *(†)*
- Songhees (a.k.a. Ləkʷəŋíriəŋ) *(†)*

11. **Twana** (a.k.a. Skokomish, Sqʷuqʷúʔbəšq, Tuwáduqutšad) *(†)*

- Quilcene
- Skokomish (a.k.a. Sqʷuqʷúʔbəšq)

B. Tsamosan (a.k.a. Olympic)

i. Inland

12. **Cowlitz** (a.k.a. Lower Cowlitz, Sx̌púlmš) *(†)*

13. **Upper Chehalis** (a.k.a. Q̓ʷaẏáyitq̓) *(†)*

- Oakville Chehalis
- Satsop
- Tenino Chehalis

ii. Maritime

14. **Lower Chehalis** (a.k.a. təẃálməš) *(†)*

- Humptulips
- Westport-Shoalwater
- Wynoochee

15. **Quinault** (a.k.a. Kʷínayt)

- Queets
- Quinault

C. Tillamook

16. **Tillamook** (a.k.a. Hutyéyu) *(†)*

Siletz

- Siletz

Tillamook

- Garibaldi-Nestucca
- Nehalem

Interior Salish

A. Northern

17. Shuswap (a.k.a. Secwepemctsín, səxwəpməxcín)

Eastern

- Kinbasket
- Shuswap Lake

Western

- Canim Lake
- Chu Chua
- Deadman's Creek–Kamloops
- Fraser River
- Pavilion-Bonaparte

18. St'at'imcets (a.k.a. Lillooet, Lilloet, St'át'imcets)

- Lillooet-Fountain
- Mount Currie–Douglas

19. Thompson River Salish (a.k.a. Nlaka'pamux, Ntlakapmuk, nɬeʔkepmxcín, Thompson River, Thompson Salish, Thompson, known in frontier times as the Hakamaugh, Klackarpun, Couteau or Knife Indians)

- Lytton
- Nicola Valley
- Spuzzum–Boston Bar
- Thompson Canyon

B. Southern

20. Coeur d'Alene (a.k.a. Snchitsu'umshtsn, snčícuʔumšcn)

21. Columbia-Moses (a.k.a. Columbia, Nxaʔamxcín)

- Chelan
- Entiat
- Columbian
- Wenatchee (a.k.a. Pesquous)

22. Colville-Okanagan (a.k.a. Okanagan, Nsilxcín, Nsíylxcən, ta nukunaqínxcən)

Northern

- Quilchena & Spaxomin[2]
- Arrow Lakes
- Penticton
- Similkameen
- Vernon

Southern

- Colville-Inchelium
- Methow
- San Poil–Nespelem
- Southern Okanogan

23. Spokane-Kalispel-Bitterroot Salish-Upper Pend d'Oreille

- Salish (a.k.a. Séliš, Bitterroot Salish, Flathead)

- Kalispel (a.k.a. Qalispé)
  - Chewelah
  - Kalispel (a.k.a. Qlispé, Lower Pend d'Oreille, Lower Kalispel)
  - Upper Pend d'Oreile (a.k.a. Čłqetkʷmcin, Qlispé)
- Spokane (a.k.a. Npoqíništcn)

Pentlatch, Nooksack, Twana, Lower Chehalis, Upper Chehalis, Cowlitz, and Tillamook are now extinct. Additionally, the Lummi, Semiahmoo, Songhees, and Sooke dialects of Northern Straits are also extinct.

Genetic relations

No relationship to any other language is well established. The most plausible connection is with the language isolate Kutenai (Kootenai), which is generally considered not unlikely but not solidly established.

Edward Sapir suggested that the Salishan languages may be related to the Wakashan and Chimakuan languages in a hypothetical Mosan family. This proposal persists primarily due to Sapir's stature. There is little evidence for it and no progress has been made in reconstructing such a family.[3]

The Salishan languages, principally Chehalis, contributed greatly to the vocabulary of the Chinook Jargon.

Family features

- post-velar harmony (more areal)
- presence of syllables without vowels
- grammatical reduplication
- nonconcatenation (infixes, metathesis, glottalization)
- tenselessness
- nounlessness (controversial)

In popular culture

Stanley Evans has written a series of crime fiction novels that use Salish lore and language.

An episode of Stargate SG-1 ("Spirits", 2x13) features a culture of extraterrestrial humans loosely inspired by Pacific coastal First Nations culture, and who speak a language referred to as "ancient Salish".

Bibliography

- Beck, David. (2000). Grammatical convergence and the genesis of diversity in the Northwest Coast Sprachbund. *Anthropological Linguistics* 42, 147–213.
- Boas, Franz, et al. (1917). *Folk-Tales of Salishan and Sahaptin Tribes*. Memoirs of the American Folk-lore Society, 11. Lancaster, Pa: American Folk-Lore Society.
- Czaykowska-Higgins, Ewa; & Kinkade, M. Dale (Eds.). (1997). *Salish languages and linguistics: Theoretical and descriptive perspectives*. Berlin: Mouton de Gruyter. ISBN 3-11-015492-7.
- Flathead Culture Committee. (1981). *Common Names of the Flathead Language*. St. Ignatius, Mont: The Committee.
- Kroeber, Paul D. (1999). *The Salish language family: Reconstructing syntax*. Lincoln: University of Nebraska Press in cooperation with the American Indian Studies Research Institute, Indiana University, Bloomington.
- Kuipers, Aert H. (2002).*Salish Etymological Dictionary*. Missoula, MT: Linguistics Laboratory, University of Montana. ISBN 1879763168
- Liedtke, Stefan. (1995). *Wakashan, Salishan and Penutian and Wider Connections Cognate Sets*. Linguistic data on diskette series, no. 09. Munchen: Lincom Europa,z\v1995.

- Pilling, James Constantine. (1893). *Bibliography of the Salishan Languages.* Washington: G.P.O..
- Pilling, James Constantine (2007). *Bibliography of the Salishan Languages.* Reprint by Gardners Books. ISBN 9781430469278
- Thompson, Laurence C. (1973). The northwest. In T. A. Sebeok (Ed.), *Linguistics in North America* (pp. 979–1045). Current trends in linguistics (Vol. 10). The Hague: Mouton.
- Thompson, Laurence C. (1979). Salishan and the northwest. In L. Campbell & M. Mithun (Eds.), *The languages of native America: Historical and comparative assessment* (pp. 692–765). Austin: University of Texas Press.

External links

- Bibliography of Materials on Salishan Languages [4] (YDLI)
- University of Montana Occasional Papers in Linguistics (UMOPL) [5] (Native languages of the Northwest)
- Coast Salish Culture: an Outline Bibliography [6]
- Coast Salish Collections [7]
- International Conference on Salish and Neighboring Languages [8]
- The Salishan Studies List [9] (Linguist List)
- Native Peoples, Plants & Animals: Halkomelem [10]
- Saanich [11] (Timothy Montler's site)
- Klallam [12] (Timothy Montler's site)
- A Bibliography of Northwest Coast Linguistics [13]
- Classification of the Salishan languages reflecting current scholarship [14]
- Ethnologue classification for Salishan [15]
- Nkwusm Salish Language Institute [16]
- Tulalip Lushootseed Language Web Site [17]
- Recordings of Montana Salish Wordlists with phonetic transcription [18] by Peter Ladefoged

References

[1] "First Nations Culture Areas Index" (http://www.civilization.ca/cmc/exhibitions/tresors/ethno/etb0170e.shtml). *the Canadian Museum of Civilization.* .
[2] (http://www.uppernicolaband.com)
[3] Beck (2000).
[4] http://www.ydli.org/biblios/salbib.htm
[5] http://grizzly.umt.edu/ling/umopl/titles.htm
[6] http://home.istar.ca/~bthom/salish-rev.htm
[7] http://collections.ic.gc.ca/salish/ph2/trad/salish.htm
[8] http://www.cas.unt.edu/~montler/salishan/icsnl.htm
[9] http://listserv.linguistlist.org/archives/salishan.html
[10] http://www.sfu.ca/halk-ethnobiology/
[11] http://www.ling.unt.edu/~montler/Saanich/
[12] http://www.ling.unt.edu/~montler/Klallam/index.htm
[13] http://www.lib.montana.edu/~bcoon/nwcst.html
[14] http://www.ydli.org/bcother/bclist.htm#sal
[15] http://www.ethnologue.com/show_family.asp?subid=91083
[16] http://www.salishworld.com/
[17] http://www.tulaliplushootseed.com/
[18] http://archive.phonetics.ucla.edu/Language/FLA/FLA.html

Lower Similkameen Indian Band

The **Lower Similkameen Indian Band** is a First Nations government in the Canadian province of British Columbia, located in the town of Keremeos in the Similkameen District. They are a member of the Okanagan Nation Alliance.

See also
• Okanagan people

Upper Similkameen Indian Band

The **Upper Similkameen Indian Band** is a First Nations government in the Canadian province of British Columbia, located in town of Keremeos in the Similkameen District. They are a member of the Okanagan Nation Alliance.

See also
• Okanagan people

Westbank First Nation

The **Westbank First Nation** is a First Nations government in the Okanagan region of the Canadian province of British Columbia, located with the District of West Kelowna. They are a member of the Okanagan Nation Alliance. The Westbank First Nation is one of the most progressive, successful First Nations in Canada. Having achieved Self-Government in 2005 they have experienced unparalleled and explosive growth. With a stable and sophisticated government and leased land system; large amounts of undeveloped serviced land; adjacent to Kelowna and bordering Lake Okanagan (one of the most desirable areas in Canada); commercial and residential developers are scrambling to gain a foothold for their projects on this Reserve.

Indian Reserves
Indian Reserves under the jurisdiction of the Westbank First Nation are:[1]
• Tsinstikeptum Indian Reserve No. 9, 641.8 ha., 6 miles southwest of the City of Kelowna, within the boundaries of West Kelowna
• Tsinstikeptum Indian Reserve No. 10, 339 ha., immediately opposite the City of Kelowna, within the boundaries of West Kelowna. This reserve is what is usually meant by the phrase "Westbank Indian Reserve"
• Medicine Creek Indian Reserve No. 12, 662.50 ha., 10 km southeast of Kelowna
• Medicine Hill Indian Reserve No. 11, 515.70 ha., 15 km southeast of Kelowna
• Mission Creek Indian Reserve No. 8, 2 ha., on left bank of Mission Creek 1 mile from Okanagan Lake, 2 miles south of downtown Kelowna

See also

- Okanagan people

External links

- Westbank First Nation website [2]
- Westbank First Nation Forestry website [3]

References

[1] Indian and Northern Affairs Canada, Reserves/Villagse/Settlements detail for Westbank First Nation (http://pse5-esd5.ainc-inac.gc.ca/fnp/
     Main/Search/FNReserves.aspx?BAND_NUMBER=601&lang=eng)

[2] http://www.wfn.ca/

[3] http://www.wfndc.ca/

Osoyoos Indian Band

The **Osoyoos Indian Band** is a First Nations government in the Canadian province of British Columbia, located in the town of Osoyoos in the Okanagan valley, about four kilometres north of the International Border. They are a member of the Okanagan Nation Alliance.

The band has established the Nk'mip Desert Cultural Centre on the east side of Osoyoos. The centre gives tours in the arid region (which is not really a desert, but a shrub steppe) and explains the uniqueness of plant species found there. The band have also established a vineyard and various other economic development undertakings.

See also

- Okanagan people

External links

- Osoyoos Indian Band website [1]
- Osoyoos Indian Band Development Corporation [2] (band-owned businesses)

References

[1] http://www.oib.ca

[2] http://www.oib.ca/oldsite/business.htm

Penticton Indian Band

The **Penticton Indian Band** is a First Nations government in the Canadian province of British Columbia, located next to the city of Penticton in the Okanagan valley. They are a member of the Okanagan Nation Alliance.

See also
• Okanagan people

Okanagan Indian Band

The **Okanagan Indian Band** is a First Nations government in the Canadian province of British Columbia, located in the city of Vernon in the Okanagan valley. They are a member of the Okanagan Nation Alliance.

On February 22, 2010 the Okanagan Indian Band began blockading Tolko Industries Ltd.'s access to the Browns Creek watershed.[1] The blockade is supported by the Union of BC Indian Chiefs.[2]

See also
• Okanagan people

External links
• Okanagan Indian Band Website [3]

References
[1] B.C. band fights logging on site of land claim (http://www.cbc.ca/canada/british-columbia/story/2010/02/22/
    bc-okanagan-tolko-logging-land-claim.html)
[2] Union of BC Indian Chiefs Supports Okanagan Indian Band in Browns Creek Faceoff (http://www.ubcic.bc.ca/News_Releases/
    UBCICNews02211001.htm)
[3] http://www.okib.ca/

Okanagan people

Okanagan
Regions with significant populations
Pacific Northwest
Languages
English, Interior Salishan
Related ethnic groups
Colville, Sanpoil, Nespelem, Sinixt, Wenatchi, Entiat, Methow, Palus, Sinkiuse-Columbia, and the Nez Perce of Chief Joseph's Band peoples

The **Okanagan** people, also spelled **Okanogan**, are a First Nations and Native American people whose traditional territory spans the U.S.-Canada boundary in Washington state and British Columbia. Known in their own language as the **Syilx**, they are part of the Interior Salish ethnological and linguistic groupings, the Okanagan are closely related to the Spokan, Sinixt, Nez Perce, Pend Oreille, Shuswap and Nlaka'pamux peoples in the same region.

When the Oregon Treaty partitioned the Pacific Northwest in 1846, the portion of the tribe remaining in what became Washington Territory reorganized under Chief Tonasket as a separate group from the majority of the Okanagans, whose communities remain in Canada. The Okanagan Tribal Alliance, however, also incorporates the American branch of the Okanagans, who are part of the Confederated Tribes of the Colville, a multi-tribal government in Washington state.

The bounds of Okanagan territory are roughly the basin of Okanagan Lake and the Okanagan River, plus the basin of the Similkameen River to the west of the Okanagan valley, and some of the uppermost valley of the Nicola River. The various

Okanagan family, c1918

Okanagan communities in British Columbia and Washington form the Okanagan Nation Alliance, a border-spanning organization which includes American-side Okanogans resident in the Colville Indian Reservation, where the Okanagan people are sometimes known as Colvilles.

A group of Okanagan people in the Nicola Valley, which is at the northwestern perimeter of Okanagan territory, are known in their dialect as the Spaxomin, and are joint members in a historic alliance with neighbouring communities of the Nlaka'pamux in the region known as the Nicola Country, which is named after the 19th Century chief who founded the alliance, Nicola. This alliance today is manifested in the Nicola Tribal Association.

Governments

- Okanagan Nation Alliance
  - Westbank First Nation (Kelowna)
  - Lower Similkameen Indian Band (Keremeos)
  - Upper Similkameen Indian Band (Keremeos)
  - Osoyoos Indian Band
  - Penticton Indian Band
  - Okanagan Indian Band (Vernon)
  - Upper Nicola Indian Band (Merritt) - also part of the Nicola Tribal Association
  - Conferated Tribes of the Colville

See also

- Okanagan Trail
- Chief Nicola
- Okanagan Mourning Dove
- Mourning Dove (author)

Further reading

- Boas, Franz (1917). *Folk-tales of Salishan and Sahaptin tribes.* Published for the American Folk-Lore Society by G.E. Stechert & Co..Available online through the Washington State Library's Classics in Washington History collection [1] Includes: *Okanagon tales* by James A. Teit and *Okanagon tales* by Marian K. Gould.
- Carstens, Peter. *The Queen's People: A Study of Hegemony, Coercion, and Accommodation Among the Okanagan of Canada.* Toronto: University of Toronto Press, 1991. ISBN 0802058930
- Robinson, Harry, and Wendy C. Wickwire. *Nature Power: In the Spirit of an Okanagan Storyteller.* Vancouver: Douglas & McIntyre, 1992. ISBN 1550540602

External links

- Map of Okanagan territory [2]
- Okanagan Tribal Alliance Homepage [3]
  - "Original People", a Syilx account of their history [4]
  - Westbank First Nation homepage [5]
  - Okanagan Indian Band homepage [6]
  - Penticton Indian Band homepage [7]
  - Osoyoos Indian Band homepage [1]
  - Lower Similkameen Indian Band homepage [8]
  - Upper Nicola Indian Band homepage [9]
  - Conferated Tribes of the Colville homepage [10]

Legends and traditional stories

- Creation of the animal people: Okanagan creation myth [11]
- The bear woman: Okanagan legend about a woman kidnapped by a grizzly bear [12]
- Dirty boy: Okanagan legend about a woman who married the sun [13]

References

[1] http://www.secstate.wa.gov/history/publications_detail.aspx?p=42
[2] http://wfn.ca/local_government/ONAmap.jpg
[3] http://www.syilx.org
[4] http://www.syilx.org/history-origin.php
[5] http://wfn.ca
[6] http://www.okanagan.org
[7] http://www.pib.ca
[8] http://www.lsib.org
[9] http://www.uppernicolaband.com
[10] http://www.colvilletribes.com
[11] http://pyramidmesa.netfirms.com/okanogan1.html
[12] http://www.pitt.edu/~dash/animalindian.html#bearwoman
[13] http://www.firstpeople.us/FP-Html-Legends/DirtyBoy-Okanagon.html

Okanagan Nation Alliance

The **Okanagan Nation Alliance** is a First Nations Tribal Council in the Canadian province of British Columbia, spanning the Nicola, Okanagan and Similkameen Districts of the Canadian province of British Columbia and also the Colville Indian Reservation in Washington state.

Member Governments

- Okanagan Nation Alliance
  - Westbank First Nation (West Kelowna)
  - Lower Similkameen Indian Band (in Keremeos)
  - Upper Similkameen Indian Band (in Princeton)
  - Osoyoos Indian Band
  - Penticton Indian Band
  - Okanagan Indian Band (in Vernon)
  - Upper Nicola Indian Band (near Merritt) - also part of the Nicola Tribal Association
  - Confederated Tribes of the Colville

See also

- Okanagan people
- List of tribal councils in British Columbia

External links

- Map of Okanagan territory [1]
- Okanagan Tribal Alliance Homepage [3]
  - "Original People", a Syilx account of their history [4]
  - Westbank First Nation homepage [2]
  - Okanagan Indian Band homepage [2]
  - Penticton Indian Band homepage [7]
  - Osoyoos Indian Band homepage [1]
  - Lower Similkameen Indian Band homepage [8]
  - Upper Nicola Indian Band homepage [9]

- Conferated Tribes of the Colville homepage [10]

References

[1] http://www.okib.ca/history/territory.php

[2] http://www.okib.ca

Canada

Canada	
Motto: *A Mari Usque Ad Mare* (Latin) "From Sea to Sea"	
Anthem: "O Canada" **Royal anthem:** "God Save the Queen"[1] [2]	
Capital	Ottawa 45°24′N 75°40′W
Largest city	Toronto
Official language(s)	English and French
Recognised regional languages	Inuktitut, Inuinnaqtun, Cree, Dëne Sųłiné, Gwich'in, Inuvialuktun, Slavey and Tłįchǫ Yatiì[3]
Demonym	Canadian
Government	Federation, parliamentary democracy, and constitutional monarchy[4]
- Monarch	HM Queen Elizabeth II
- Governor General	Michaëlle Jean
- Prime Minister	Stephen Harper
Legislature	Parliament
- Upper House	Senate

-	Lower House	House of Commons
	**Establishment**	
-	British North America Acts	July 1, 1867
-	Statute of Westminster	December 11, 1931
-	Canada Act	April 17, 1982
	**Area**	
-	Total	9,984,670 km^2 (2nd) 3,854,085 sq mi
-	Water (%)	8.92 (891,163 km²/344,080 mi²)
	**Population**	
-	2010 estimate	34199000[5] (36th)
-	2006 census	31,241,030[6]
-	Density	3.41/km^2 (228th) 8.3/sq mi
GDP (PPP)		2009 estimate
-	Total	$1.281 trillion[7]
-	Per capita	$38,025[7]
GDP (nominal)		2009 estimate
-	Total	$1.336 trillion[7]
-	Per capita	$39,668[7]
Gini		32.1 (2005)[8]
HDI (2009)		▲ 0.966[9] (very high) (4th)
Currency		Canadian Dollar ($) (CAD)
Time zone		(UTC−3.5 to −8)
-	Summer (DST)	(UTC−2.5 to −7)
Date formats		dd-mm-yyyy, mm-dd-yyyy, and yyyy-mm-dd (CE)
Drives on the		Right
Internet TLD		.ca
Calling code		+1
Canada portal		

Canada (🔊 /ˈkænədə/) is a country occupying most of northern North America, extending from the Atlantic Ocean in the east to the Pacific Ocean in the west and northward into the Arctic Ocean. It is the world's second largest country by total area. Canada's common border with the United States to the south and northwest is the longest in the world.

The land occupied by Canada was inhabited for millennia by various groups of Aboriginal peoples. Beginning in the late 15th century, British and French expeditions explored, and later settled, along the Atlantic coast. France ceded nearly all of its colonies in North America in 1763 after the Seven Years' War. In 1867, with the union of three British North American colonies through Confederation, Canada was formed as a federal dominion of four provinces.[10] [11] This began an accretion of provinces and territories and a process of increasing autonomy from the United Kingdom. This widening autonomy was highlighted by the Statute of Westminster of 1931 and culminated in the Canada Act of 1982, which severed the vestiges of legal dependence on the British parliament.

A federation consisting of ten provinces and three territories, Canada is governed as a parliamentary democracy and a constitutional monarchy with Queen Elizabeth II as its head of state. It is a bilingual nation with both English and French as official languages at the federal level. One of the world's highly developed countries, Canada has a diversified economy that is reliant upon its abundant natural resources and upon trade—particularly with the United States, with which Canada has had a long and complex relationship. It is a member of the G8, G-20, NATO, OECD, WTO, Commonwealth, Francophonie, OAS, APEC, and UN.

Etymology

The name *Canada* comes from a St. Lawrence Iroquoian word, *kanata*, meaning "village" or "settlement".[12] In 1535, indigenous inhabitants of the present-day Quebec City region used the word to direct French explorer Jacques Cartier towards the village of Stadacona.[13] Cartier later used the word *Canada* to refer not only to that particular village, but also the entire area subject to Donnacona (the chief at Stadacona); by 1545, European books and maps had begun referring to this region as *Canada*.[13]

From the early 17th century onwards, that part of New France that lay along the Saint Lawrence River and the northern shores of the Great Lakes was known as *Canada*. The area was later split into two British colonies, Upper Canada and Lower Canada. They were re-unified as the Province of Canada in 1841.[14] Upon Confederation in 1867, the name *Canada* was adopted as the legal name for the new country, and *Dominion* (a term from Psalm 72:8)[15] was conferred as the country's title. Combined, the term *Dominion of Canada* was in common usage until the 1950s.[16] As Canada asserted its political autonomy from the United Kingdom, the federal government increasingly used simply *Canada* on state documents and treaties, a change that was reflected in the renaming of the national holiday from Dominion Day to Canada Day in 1982.[16]

History

Aboriginal peoples

Archaeological and Indigenous genetic studies support a human presence in the northern Yukon from 26,500 years ago, and in southern Ontario from 9,500 years ago.[17] [18] [19] Old Crow Flats and Bluefish Caves are two of the earliest archaeological sites of human (Paleo-Indians) habitation in Canada.[20] [21] [22] Among the First Nations peoples, there are eight unique stories of creation and their adaptations.These are the earth diver, world parent, emergence, conflict, robbery, rebirth of corpse, two creators and their contests, and the brother myth.[23] The characteristics of Canadian Aboriginal civilizations included permanent or urban settlements, agriculture, civic and monumental architecture, and complex societal hierarchies.[24] Some of these civilisations had long faded by the time of the first permanent European arrivals (c. late 15th–early 16th centuries), and have been discovered through archaeological investigations.

The aboriginal population is estimated to have been between 200,000[25] and two million in the late 1400s,[26] with a figure of 500,000 currently accepted by Canada's Royal Commission on Aboriginal Health.[27] Repeated outbreaks of European infectious diseases such as influenza, measles and smallpox (to which they had no natural immunity), combined with other effects of European contact, resulted in a forty to eighty percent aboriginal population decrease post-contact.[25] Aboriginal peoples in Canada include the First Nations,[28] Inuit,[29] and Métis.[30] The Métis a culture of mixed blood originated in the mid-17th century when First Nation and Inuit married European settlers.[31] The Inuit had more limited interaction with European settlers during the early periods.[32]

European colonization

Benjamin West's *The Death of General Wolfe*
(1771) dramatizes Wolfe's death during the Battle
of the Plains of Abraham at Quebec in 1759; the
battle was part of the Seven Years' War

Europeans first arrived when Norse sailors (often referred to as Vikings) settled briefly at L'Anse aux Meadows in Newfoundland around 1000;[33] [34] after the failure of that colony, there was no known further attempt at Canadian exploration until 1497, when Italian seafarer Giovanni Caboto (John Cabot) explored Canada's Atlantic coast for England.[35] Subsequently, between 1498 and 1521, various Portuguese mariners reconoittered eastern Canada and established fishing posts in the region.[36] In 1534 Jacques Cartier explored Canada for France.[37] French explorer Samuel de Champlain arrived in 1603 and established the first permanent European settlements at Port Royal in 1605 and Quebec City in 1608.[38] Among French colonists of New France, *Canadiens* extensively settled the Saint Lawrence River valley and Acadians settled the present-day Maritimes, while French fur traders and Catholic missionaries explored the Great Lakes, Hudson Bay, and the Mississippi watershed to Louisiana. The French and Iroquois Wars broke out over control of the fur trade.[39]

The English established fishing outposts in Newfoundland around 1610 and established the Thirteen Colonies to the south.[40] A series of four Intercolonial Wars erupted between 1689 and 1763.[41] Mainland Nova Scotia came under British rule with the Treaty of Utrecht (1713); the Treaty of Paris (1763) ceded Canada and most of New France to Britain after the Seven Years' War.[42]

The Royal Proclamation (1763) carved the Province of Quebec out of New France and annexed Cape Breton Island to Nova Scotia.[16] St. John's Island (now Prince Edward Island) became a separate colony in 1769.[43] To avert conflict in Quebec, the British passed the Quebec Act of 1774, expanding Quebec's territory to the Great Lakes and Ohio Valley. It re-established the French language, Catholic faith, and French civil law there. This angered many residents of the Thirteen Colonies and helped to fuel the American Revolution.[16]

The Treaty of Paris (1783) recognized American independence and ceded territories south of the Great Lakes to the United States. Around 50,000 United Empire Loyalists fled the United States to Canada.[44] New Brunswick was split from Nova Scotia as part of a reorganization of Loyalist settlements in the Maritimes. To accommodate English-speaking Loyalists in Quebec, the Constitutional Act of 1791 divided the province into French-speaking Lower Canada (later the province of Quebec) and English-speaking Upper Canada (later Ontario), granting each its own elected Legislative Assembly.[45]

Robert Harris's *Fathers of Confederation*,[46] an
amalgamation of the Charlottetown and Quebec
conferences

Canada (Upper and Lower) was the main front in the War of 1812 between the United States and the British Empire. Following the war, large-scale immigration to Canada from Britain and Ireland began in 1815.[47] From 1825 to 1846, 626,628 European immigrants landed at Canadian ports.[48] Between one-quarter and one-third of all Europeans who immigrated to Canada before 1891 died of infectious diseases.[25] The timber industry surpassed the fur trade in economic importance in the early nineteenth century.

The desire for responsible government resulted in the aborted Rebellions of 1837. The Durham Report subsequently recommended responsible government and the assimilation of French Canadians into British culture.[16] The Act of Union 1840 merged The Canadas into a united Province of Canada. Responsible government was established for all British North American provinces by 1849.[49] The signing of the Oregon Treaty by Britain and the United States in 1846 ended the Oregon boundary dispute, extending the border westward along the 49th parallel. This paved the way for British colonies on Vancouver Island (1849) and in British Columbia (1858).[50] Canada launched a series of exploratory expeditions to claim Rupert's Land and the Arctic region.

Confederation and expansion

Following several constitutional conferences, the Constitution Act, 1867 officially proclaimed Canadian Confederation, creating "one Dominion under the name of Canada" on July 1, 1867, with four provinces: Ontario, Quebec, Nova Scotia, and New Brunswick.[10] [51] Canada assumed control of Rupert's Land and the North-Western Territory to form the Northwest Territories, where the Métis' grievances ignited the Red River Rebellion and the creation of the province of Manitoba in July 1870.[52] British Columbia and Vancouver Island (which had united in 1866) and the colony of Prince Edward Island joined the Confederation in 1871 and 1873, respectively.[53] Prime Minister John A. Macdonald's Conservative government established a national policy of tariffs to protect nascent Canadian manufacturing industries.[54]

An animated map, exhibiting the growth and change of Canada's provinces and territories since Confederation

To open the West, the government sponsored construction of three trans-continental railways (including the Canadian Pacific Railway), opened the prairies to settlement with the Dominion Lands Act, and established the North-West Mounted Police to assert its authority over this territory.[55] [56] In 1898, after the Klondike Gold Rush in the Northwest Territories, the Canadian government created the Yukon territory. Under Liberal Prime Minister Wilfrid Laurier, continental European immigrants settled the prairies, and Alberta and Saskatchewan became provinces in 1905.[53]

Early 20th century

Canadian soldiers at the Battle of Vimy Ridge in 1917

Because Britain still maintained control of Canada's foreign affairs under the Confederation Act, its declaration of war in 1914 automatically brought Canada into World War I.[57] Volunteers sent to the Western Front later became part of the Canadian Corps.[57] The Corps played a substantial role in the Battle of Vimy Ridge and other major battles of the war.[57] Out of approximately 625,000 who served, about 60,000 were killed and another 173,000 were wounded.[58] The Conscription Crisis of 1917 erupted when conservative Prime Minister Robert Borden brought in compulsory military service over the objection of French-speaking Quebecers.[57] In 1919, Canada joined the League of Nations independently of Britain[57] and in 1931, the Statute of Westminster affirmed Canada's independence.[59]

The Great Depression brought economic hardship all over Canada. In response, the Co-operative Commonwealth Federation (CCF) in Alberta and Saskatchewan enacted many measures of a welfare state (as pioneered by Tommy Douglas) into the 1940s and 1950s.[60] Canada declared war on Germany independently during World War II under Liberal Prime Minister William Lyon Mackenzie King, three days after Britain. The first Canadian Army units arrived in Britain in December 1939.[57]

Canadian troops played important roles in the failed 1942 Dieppe Raid in France, the Allied invasion of Italy, the D-Day landings, the Battle of Normandy, and the Battle of the Scheldt in 1944.[57] Canada provided asylum and protection for the monarchy of the Netherlands while that country was occupied, and is credited by the country for leadership and major contribution to its liberation from Nazi Germany.[61] The Canadian economy boomed as industry manufactured military materiel for Canada, Britain, China, and the Soviet Union. Despite another Conscription Crisis in Quebec, Canada finished the war with one of the largest armed forces in the world, and the second-wealthiest economy.[62] [63] In 1945, during the war, Canada became one of the founding members of the United Nations.[57]

Modern times

The Dominion of Newfoundland (now Newfoundland and Labrador), at the time equivalent in status to Canada and Australia as a Dominion, joined Canada in 1949.[64] Canada's growth, combined with the policies of successive Liberal governments, led to the emergence of a new Canadian identity, marked by the adoption of the current Maple Leaf Flag in 1965,[65] the implementation of official bilingualism (English and French) in 1969,[66] and official multiculturalism in 1971.[67] There was also the founding of socially democratic programmes, such as universal health care, the Canada Pension Plan, and Canada Student Loans, though provincial governments, particularly Quebec and Alberta, opposed many of these as incursions into their jurisdictions.[68] Finally, another series of constitutional conferences resulted in the 1982 patriation of Canada's constitution from the United Kingdom, concurrent with the creation of the Charter of Rights and Freedoms.[69] In 1999, Nunavut became Canada's third territory after a series of negotiations with the federal government.[70]

Pte. Patrick Cloutier, a 'Van Doo' perimeter sentry, and Mohawk Warrior Brad Larocque, a University of Saskatchewan economics student, face off during the Oka Crisis[71]

At the same time, Quebec was undergoing profound social and economic changes through the Quiet Revolution, giving birth to a nationalist movement in the province and the more radical Front de libération du Québec (FLQ), whose actions ignited the October Crisis in 1970.[72] A decade later, an unsuccessful referendum on sovereignty-association was held in 1980,[72] after which attempts at constitutional amendment failed in 1990. A second referendum followed in 1995, in which sovereignty was rejected by a slimmer margin of just 50.6% to 49.4%.[73] In 1997, the Supreme Court ruled that unilateral secession by a province would be unconstitutional, and the Clarity Act was passed by parliament, outlining the terms of a negotiated departure from Confederation.[73]

In addition to the issues of Quebec sovereignty, a number of crises shook Canadian society in the late 1980s and early 1990s. These included the explosion of Air India Flight 182 in 1985, the largest mass murder in Canadian history;[74] the École Polytechnique massacre in 1989, a university shooting targeting female students;[75] and the Oka Crisis in 1990,[76] the first of a number of violent confrontations between the government and Aboriginal groups.[77] Canada also joined the Gulf War in 1990 as part of a US-led coalition force, and was active in several peacekeeping missions in the late 1990s.[78] It sent troops to Afghanistan in 2001, but declined to send forces to Iraq when the US invaded in 2003.[79]

Government and politics

Canada has strong democratic traditions upheld through a parliamentary government within the construct of constitutional monarchy, the monarchy of Canada being the foundation of the executive, legislative, and judicial branches and its authority stemming from the Canadian populace.[80] [81] [82] [83] The sovereign is Queen Elizabeth II, who also serves as head of state of 15 other Commonwealth countries and resides predominantly in the United Kingdom. As such, the Queen's representative, the Governor General of Canada (presently Michaëlle Jean[84]), carries out most of the royal duties in Canada.[85]

Parliament Hill in Canada's capital, Ottawa

The direct participation of the royal and viceroyal figures in any of these areas of governance is limited, though;[83] [86] [87] [88] in practice, their use of the executive powers is directed by the Cabinet, a committee of ministers of the Crown responsible to the elected House of Commons and headed by the Prime Minister of Canada (presently Stephen Harper[89]), the head of government. To ensure the stability of government, the governor general will usually appoint as prime minister the person who is the current leader of the political party that can obtain the confidence of a plurality in the House of Commons and the prime minister chooses the Cabinet.[90] The Prime Minister's Office (PMO) is thus one of the most powerful institutions in government, initiating most legislation for parliamentary approval and selecting for appointment by the Crown, besides the aforementioned, the governor general, lieutenant governors, senators, federal court judges, and heads of crown corporations and government agencies.[91] The leader of the party with the second-most seats usually becomes the Leader of Her Majesty's Loyal Opposition (presently Michael Ignatieff[92]) and is part of an adversarial parliamentary system intended to keep the government in check.

The Senate chamber within the Centre Block on Parliament Hill

Each Member of Parliament in the House of Commons is elected by simple majority in an electoral district or riding. General elections must be called by the governor general, on the advice of the prime minister, within four years of the previous election, or may be triggered by the government losing a confidence vote in the House.[93] Members of the Senate, whose seats are apportioned on a regional basis, serve until age 75.[94] Four parties had representatives elected to the federal parliament in the 2008 elections: the Conservative Party of Canada (governing party), the Liberal Party of Canada (the Official Opposition), the New Democratic Party (NDP), and the Bloc Québécois. The list of historical parties with elected representation is substantial.

Canada's federal structure divides government responsibilities between the federal government and the ten provinces. Provincial legislatures are unicameral and operate in parliamentary fashion similar to the House of Commons.[95] Canada's three territories also have legislatures, but these are not sovereign and have fewer constitutional responsibilities than the provinces and with some structural differences.[96] [97] [98]

Law

The Constitution of Canada is the supreme law of the country, and consists of written text and unwritten conventions.[99] The Constitution Act, 1867 (known as the British North America Act prior to 1982) affirmed governance based on parliamentary precedent "similar in principle to that of the United Kingdom"[100] and divided powers between the federal and provincial governments; the Statute of Westminster, 1931 granted full autonomy; and the Constitution Act, 1982 added the Canadian Charter of Rights and Freedoms, which guarantees basic rights and freedoms that usually cannot be overridden by any level of government—though a *notwithstanding clause* allows the federal parliament and provincial legislatures to override certain sections of the Charter for a period of five years—and added a constitutional amending formula.[99]

Although not without conflict, European Canadians' early interactions with First Nations and Inuit populations were relatively peaceful. Combined with Canada's late economic development in many regions, this peaceful history has allowed Canadian Indigenous peoples to have a relatively strong influence on the national culture while preserving their own identity.[101] The Canadian Crown and Aboriginal peoples began interactions during the European colonialisation period. Numbered treaties, the Indian Act, the Constitution Act of 1982 and case laws were established.[102] A series of eleven treaties were signed between Aboriginals in Canada and the reigning Monarch of Canada from 1871 to 1921.[103] These treaties are agreements with the

The Indian Chiefs Medal, presented to commemorate Treaties 3, 4, 5, 6 and 7, bearing the effigy of Queen Victoria

Government of Canada administered by Canadian Aboriginal law and overseen by the Minister of Indian Affairs and Northern Development. The role of the treaties was reaffirmed by Section Thirty-five of the Constitution Act, 1982, which "recognizes and affirms existing Aboriginal and treaty rights".[102] These rights may include provision of services such as health care, and exemption from taxation.[104] The legal and policy framework within which Canada and First Nations operate was further formalised in 2005, through the *First Nations–Federal Crown Political Accord*, which established cooperation as "a cornerstone for partnership between Canada and First Nations".[102]

The Supreme Court of Canada in Ottawa, west of Parliament Hill

Canada's judiciary plays an important role in interpreting laws and has the power to strike down laws that violate the Constitution. The Supreme Court of Canada is the highest court and final arbiter and has been led by the Right Honourable Madam Chief Justice Beverley McLachlin, P.C. (the first female Chief Justice) since 2000.[105] Its nine members are appointed by the governor general on the advice of the Prime Minister and Minister of Justice. All judges at the superior and appellate levels are appointed after consultation with nongovernmental legal bodies. The federal cabinet also appoints justices to superior courts at the provincial and territorial levels. Judicial posts at the lower provincial and territorial levels are filled by their respective governments.[106]

Common law prevails everywhere except in Quebec, where civil law predominates.[107] Criminal law is solely a federal responsibility and is uniform throughout Canada.[107] Law enforcement, including criminal courts, is a provincial responsibility, but in rural areas of all provinces except Ontario and Quebec, policing is contracted to the federal Royal Canadian Mounted Police.[108]

Foreign relations and military

Canada and the United States share the world's longest undefended border, co-operate on military campaigns and exercises, and are each other's largest trading partner.[109] Canada nevertheless has an independent foreign policy, most notably maintaining full relations with Cuba and declining to participate in the Iraq War. Canada also maintains historic ties to the United Kingdom and France and to other former British and French colonies through Canada's membership in the Commonwealth of Nations and the Francophonie.[110] Canada is noted for having a strong and positive relationship with the Netherlands, and the Dutch government traditionally gives tulips, a symbol of the Netherlands, to Canada each year in remembrance of the latter country's contribution to its liberation.[61]

A Canadian CF-18 Hornet in Cold Lake, Alberta. CF-18s have supported NORAD air sovereignty patrols and participated in combat during the Gulf War and the Kosovo and Bosnia crises.

Canada currently employs a professional, volunteer military force of about 67,000 regular and 26,000 reserve personnel.[111] The unified Canadian Forces (CF) comprise the army, navy, and air force.

Canada is an industrial nation with a highly developed science and technology sector. Since the First World War, Canada has produced its own infantry fighting vehicle, anti-tank guided missile and small arms for the Canadian Forces and particularly for the army. The Canadian Forces operate state of the art equipments able to handle modern threats through 2030–2035. Despite the financial cut between 1987–2004,[112] the Canadian Forces are well equipped. The Land Force Command currently operate approximatively 10 500 utility vehicles including G-wagon and 7000-MV and also operate approximatively 2 700 armoured fighting vehicles including the LAV-III and the Leopard 2.[113] The land force also operate approximatively 150 field artillery including the M777 howitzer and the LG1 Mark II. The Canadian navy currently operates 33 combat vessels.[114] These include the Halifax class frigate and the Victoria class submarine. The Canadian air force operates 333 aircraft.[115] These include the CF-188 Hornet, CC-130 Hercule and the CH-146 Griffon.

Strong attachment to the British Empire and Commonwealth led to major participation in British military efforts in the Second Boer War, the First World War, and the Second World War. Since then, Canada has been an advocate for multilateralism, making efforts to resolve global issues in collaboration with other nations.[116] [117] Canada was a founding member of the United Nations in 1945 and of NATO in 1949. During the Cold War, Canada was a major contributor to UN forces in the Korean War and founded the North American Aerospace Defense Command (NORAD) in cooperation with the United States to defend against potential aerial attacks from the Soviet Union.[118]

The *Halifax*-class frigate HMCS *Regina, a warship of the Canadian Navy in 2004*

During the Suez Crisis of 1956, future Prime Minister Lester B. Pearson eased tensions by proposing the inception of the United Nations Peacekeeping Force, for which he was awarded the 1957 Nobel Peace Prize.[119] As this was the first UN peacekeeping mission, Pearson is often credited as the inventor of the concept. Canada has since served in 50 peacekeeping missions, including every UN peacekeeping effort until 1989,[120] and has since maintained forces in international missions in Rwanda, the former Yugoslavia, and elsewhere; Canada has sometimes faced controversy over its involvement in foreign countries, notably in the 1993 Somalia Affair.[121] The number of Canadian military personnel participating in peacekeeping missions has decreased greatly in the past two decades. As of June 30, 2006, 133 Canadians were currently serving on United Nations peacekeeping missions worldwide, including 55 Canadian military personnel, compared with 1044 military personnel as of December 31, 1996.[122] [123]

Canada joined the Organization of American States (OAS) in 1990 and hosted the OAS General Assembly in Windsor, Ontario, in June 2000 and the third Summit of the Americas in Quebec City in April 2001.[124] Canada seeks to expand its ties to Pacific Rim economies through membership in the Asia-Pacific Economic Cooperation forum (APEC).[125]

Since 2001, Canada has had troops deployed in Afghanistan as part of the U.S. stabilization force and the UN-authorized, NATO-commanded International Security Assistance Force. Canada has committed to withdraw from Kandahar Province by 2011,[126] by which time it will have spent an estimated total of $11.3 billion on the mission.[127] Canada and the U.S. continue to integrate state and provincial agencies to strengthen security along the Canada-United States border through the Western Hemisphere Travel Initiative.[128]

In February 2007, Canada, Italy, Britain, Norway, and Russia announced their funding commitments to launch a $1.5 billion project to help develop vaccines they said could save millions of lives in poor nations, and called on others to join them.[129] In August 2007, Canadian sovereignty in Arctic waters was challenged after a Russian underwater expedition to the North Pole; Canada has considered that area to be sovereign territory since 1925.[130]

Provinces and territories

Canada is a federation composed of ten provinces and three territories. In turn, these may be grouped into regions: Western Canada, Central Canada, Atlantic Canada, and Northern Canada (the latter made up of the three territories: Yukon, Northwest Territories, and Nunavut). Eastern Canada refers to Central Canada and Atlantic Canada together. Provinces have more autonomy than territories. The provinces are responsible for most of Canada's social programs (such as health care, education, and welfare) and together collect more revenue than the federal government, an almost unique structure among federations in the world. Using its spending powers, the federal government can initiate national policies in provincial areas, such as the Canada Health Act; the provinces can opt out of these, but rarely do so in practice. Equalization payments are made by the federal government to ensure that reasonably uniform standards of services and taxation are kept between the richer and poorer provinces.[131]

A clickable map of Canada exhibiting its ten provinces and three territories, and their capitals.

Canada – Political

Geography and climate

Canada occupies a major northern portion of North America, sharing the land borders with the contiguous United States to the south and the U.S. state of Alaska to the northwest, stretching from the Atlantic Ocean in the east to the Pacific Ocean in the west; to the north lies the Arctic Ocean. By total area (including its waters), Canada is the second-largest country in the world—after Russia.[8] By land area, Canada ranks fourth (land area is total area minus the area of lakes and rivers).[132]

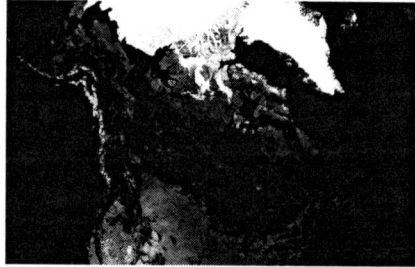

A satellite composite image of Canada.

Since 1925, Canada has claimed the portion of the Arctic between 60°W and 141°W longitude,[133] but this claim is not universally recognized. The northernmost settlement in Canada (and in the world) is Canadian Forces Station Alert on the northern tip of Ellesmere Island—latitude 82.5°N—817 kilometres (450 nautical miles, 508 miles) from the North Pole.[134] Much of the Canadian Arctic is covered by ice and permafrost. Canada also has the longest coastline in the world: 202080 kilometres (125570 mi).[8]

The population density, 3.3 inhabitants per square kilometre (8.5/sq mi), is among the lowest in the world. The most densely populated part of the country is the Quebec City – Windsor Corridor, (situated in Southern Quebec and Southern Ontario) along the Great Lakes and the Saint Lawrence River in the southeast.[135]

The Horseshoe Falls in Niagara Falls, Ontario, is one of the world's
most voluminous waterfalls,[136] renowned for both its beauty and
as a valuable source of hydroelectric power.

Canada has an extensive coastline on its north, east, and west, and since the last glacial period it has consisted of eight distinct forest regions, including extensive boreal forest on the Canadian Shield.[137] The vastness and variety of Canada's geography, ecology, vegetation and landforms have given rise to a wide variety of climates throughout the country.[138] Because of its vast size, Canada has more lakes than any other country, containing much of the world's fresh water.[139] There are also fresh-water glaciers in the Canadian Rockies and the Coast Mountains.

Average winter and summer high temperatures across Canada vary according to the location. Winters can be harsh in many regions of the country, particularly in the interior and Prairie provinces, which experience a continental climate, where daily average temperatures are near −15 °C (5 °F) but can drop below −40 °C (−40.0 °F) with severe wind chills.[140] In noncoastal regions, snow can cover the ground almost six months of the year (more in the north). Coastal British Columbia enjoys a temperate climate, with a mild and rainy winter. On the east and west coasts, average high temperatures are generally in the low 20s °C (70s °F), while between the coasts, the average summer high temperature ranges from 25 to 30 °C (77 to 86 °F), with occasional extreme heat in some interior locations exceeding 40 °C (104 °F).[141]

Canada is also geologically active, having many earthquakes and potentially active volcanoes, notably Mount Meager, Mount Garibaldi, Mount Cayley, and the Mount Edziza volcanic complex.[142] The volcanic eruption of Tseax Cone in 1775 caused a catastrophic disaster, killing 2,000 Nisga'a people and destroying their village in the Nass River valley of northern British Columbia; the eruption produced a 22.5-kilometre (14.0 mi) lava flow, and according to legend of the Nisga'a people, it blocked the flow of the Nass River.[143]

Science and technology

Canada is an industrial nation with a highly developed science and technology sector. Nearly 1.88% of Canada's GDP is allocated to research & development (R&D).[144] The country has eighteen Nobel laureates in physics, chemistry and medicine.[145] Canada ranks 12 in the world for Internet usage with 28.0 million users, 84.3% of the total population.[146]

The Canadarm in action on the Space Shuttle
Discovery during STS-116

The Defence Research and Development Canada is an agency of the Department of National Defence ,whose purpose is to respond to the scientific and technological needs of the Canadian Forces. Over the years, DRDC have been responsible for numerous innovations and inventions of practical application both in civilian and military world. These include the CADPAT, G-suit, CRV7, Carbon dioxide laser and the Flight data recorder.[147] [148] DRDC also contribute in the development of the most advanced Active Electronically Scanned Array in the world as part of an international effort involving Canada, Germany, and the Netherlands.[149]

The Canadian Space Agency conducts space, planetary, and aviation research, as well as develops rockets and satellites. In 1984, Marc Garneau became Canada's first astronaut, serving as payload specialist of STS-41-G. Canada is a participant in the International Space Station and one of the world's pioneers in space robotics with the

Canadarm, Canadarm2 and Dextre. Canada was ranked third among 20 top countries in space sciences.[150] Since the 1960s, Canada Aerospace Industries have designed and built 10 satellites, including RADARSAT-1, RADARSAT-2 and MOST.[151] Canada also produced one of the most successful sounding rockets, the Black Brant; over 1000 have been launched since they were initially produced in 1961.[152] Universities across Canada are working on the first domestic landing spacecraft: the Northern Light, designed to search for life on Mars and investigate Martian electromagnetic radiation environment and atmospheric properties. If the Northern Light is successful, Canada will be the third country to land on another planet.[153]

Economy

Canada is one of the world's wealthiest nations, with a high per-capita income, and it is a member of the Organisation for Economic Co-operation and Development (OECD) and the G8. It is one of the world's top ten trading nations.[154] Canada is a mixed market, ranking above the U.S. on the Heritage Foundation's index of economic freedom and higher than most western European nations.[155] The largest foreign importers of Canadian goods are the United States, the United Kingdom, and Japan.[156] In 2008, Canada's imported goods were worth over $442.9 billion, of which $280.8 billion was from the United States, $11.7 billion from Japan, and $11.3 billion from the United Kingdom.[156] The country's 2009 trade deficit totaled C$4.8 billion, compared with a C$46.9 billion surplus in 2008.[157]

As of October 2009, Canada's national unemployment rate was 8.6%. Provincial unemployment rates vary from a low of 5.8% in Manitoba to a high of 17% in Newfoundland and Labrador.[158] Canada's federal debt is estimated to be $566.7 billion for 2010–11, up from $463.7 billion in 2008–09.[159] Canada's net foreign debt rose by $40.6-billion to $193.8-billion in the first quarter of 2010.[160] The combined federal and provincial government deficit in the 2009–10 fiscal year could reach of $100-billion,[161] and the federal deficit is forecast to be C$49.2 billion in 2010–11.[162]

In the past century, the growth of the manufacturing, mining, and service sectors has transformed the nation from a largely rural economy to a more industrial and urban one. Like other First World nations, the Canadian economy is dominated by the service industry, which employs about three quarters of Canadians.[163] Canada is unusual among developed countries in the importance of its primary sector, in which the logging and petroleum industries are two of the most important.[164]

Current Canadian banknotes, depicting (top to bottom) Wilfrid Laurier, John A. Macdonald, Queen of Canada (Queen Elizabeth II), William Lyon Mackenzie King, and Robert Borden

Canada is one of the few developed nations that are net exporters of energy.[165] Atlantic Canada has vast offshore deposits of natural gas, and Alberta has large oil and gas resources. The immense Athabasca Oil Sands give Canada the world's second-largest oil reserves, behind Saudi Arabia.[166]

Canada is one of the world's largest suppliers of agricultural products; the Canadian Prairies are one of the most important producers of wheat, canola, and other grains.[167] Canada is the largest producer of zinc and uranium, and is a global source of many other natural resources, such as gold, nickel, aluminium, and lead.[165] Many towns in northern Canada, where agriculture is difficult, are sustainable because of nearby mines or sources of timber. Canada also has a sizable manufacturing sector centred in southern Ontario and Quebec, with automobiles and aeronautics representing particularly important industries.[168]

Representatives of the Canadian, Mexican, and United States governments sign the North American Free Trade Agreement in 1992

Economic integration with the United States has increased significantly since World War II. This has drawn the attention of Canadian nationalists, who are concerned about cultural and economic autonomy in an age of globalization, as American goods and media products have become ubiquitous.[169] The Automotive Products Trade Agreement of 1965 opened the borders to trade in the auto manufacturing industry. In the 1970s, concerns over energy self-sufficiency and foreign ownership in the manufacturing sectors prompted Prime Minister Pierre Trudeau's Liberal government to enact the National Energy Program (NEP) and the Foreign Investment Review Agency (FIRA).[170]

In the 1980s, Prime Minister Brian Mulroney's Progressive Conservatives abolished the NEP and changed the name of FIRA to "Investment Canada" in order to encourage foreign investment.[171] The Canada – United States Free Trade Agreement (FTA) of 1988 eliminated tariffs between the two countries, while the North American Free Trade Agreement (NAFTA) expanded the free-trade zone to include Mexico in the 1990s.[167] In the mid-1990s, the Liberal government under Jean Chrétien began to post annual budgetary surpluses and steadily paid down the national debt.[172] The 2008 global financial crisis caused a recession, which could boost the country's unemployment rate to 10%.[173]

Demographics

Largest metropolitan areas in Canada by population (2006 Census)					
Name	Province	Pop.	Name	Province	Pop.
Toronto	Ontario	5,113,149	Kitchener–Waterloo	Ontario	451,235
Montreal	Quebec	3,635,571	St. Catharines–Niagara	Ontario	390,317
Vancouver	British Columbia	2,116,581	Halifax	Nova Scotia	372,858
Ottawa–Gatineau	Ontario–Quebec	1,130,761	Oshawa	Ontario	330,594
Calgary	Alberta	1,079,310	Greater Victoria	British Columbia	330,088
Edmonton	Alberta	1,034,945	Windsor	Ontario	323,342
Quebec City	Quebec	715,515	Saskatoon	Saskatchewan	233,923
Winnipeg	Manitoba	694,668	Regina	Saskatchewan	194,971
Hamilton	Ontario	692,911	Sherbrooke	Quebec	186,952
London	Ontario	457,720	St. John's	Newfoundland and Labrador	181,113

Canada's 2006 census counted a total population of 31,612,897, an increase of 5.4% since 2001.[174] Population growth is from immigration and, to a lesser extent, natural growth. About four-fifths of Canada's population lives within 150 kilometres (93 mi) of the United States border.[175] A similar proportion live in urban areas concentrated in the Quebec City – Windsor Corridor (notably the Greater Golden Horseshoe, including Toronto and area, Montreal, and Ottawa), the BC Lower Mainland (consisting of the region surrounding Vancouver), and the Calgary–Edmonton Corridor in Alberta.[176]

Historical populations		
Year	Pop.	%±
1851	2415000	—
1861	3174000	31.4%
1871	3689000	16.2%
1881	4325000	17.2%
1891	4833000	11.7%
1901	5371000	11.1%
1911	7207000	34.2%
1921	8788000	21.9%
1931	10377000	18.1%
1941	11507000	10.9%
1951	14009000	21.7%
1961	18238000	30.2%
1971	21962000	20.4%
1981	24820000	13.0%
1991	28031000	12.9%
2001	31021000	10.7%
2010 est.	34199000	10.2%
Source: Statistics Canada[177]		

According to the 2006 census, the largest reported ethnic origin is English (21%), followed by French (15.8%), Scottish (15.2%), Irish (13.9%), German (10.2%), Italian (5%), Chinese (3.9%), Ukrainian (3.6%), and First Nations (3.5%). Approximately one third of respondents identified their ethnicity as "Canadian".[178] There are 600 recognized First Nations governments or bands encompassing 1,172,790 people.[179]

Canada's Aboriginal population is growing at almost twice the national rate, and 3.8% of Canada's population claimed aboriginal identity in 2006. Another 16.2% of the population belonged to non-aboriginal visible minorities.[180] The largest visible minority groups in Canada are South Asian (4%), Chinese (3.9%) and Black (2.5%).[181] In 1961, less than 2% of Canada's population (about 300,000 people) could be classified as belonging to a visible minority group and less than 1% as aboriginal.[182] In 2006, 51.0% of Vancouver's population and 46.9% of Toronto's population were members of visible minority groups.[183] [184] Between 2001 and 2006, the visible minority population rose by 27.2%.[181] According to a 2005 forecast by Statistics Canada, the proportion of Canadians belonging to a visible minority group in Canada could reach as much as 23% by 2017. As of 2007, almost one in five Canadians (19.8%) were foreign-born.[185] Nearly 60% of new immigrants hail from Asia (including the Middle East).[185] By 2031, one in three Canadians could belong to a visible minority group.[186]

Religion in Canada (2001 Census)[187]

Religion	Percent
Christianity	77.1%
No religion	16.5%
Islam	2.0%
Judaism	1.1%
Buddhism	1.0%
Hinduism	1.0%
Sikhism	0.9%

Canada has the highest per-capita immigration rate in the world, driven by economic policy and family reunification, and is aiming for between 240,000 and 265,000 new permanent residents in 2010.[188] Canada also accepts large numbers of refugees. New immigrants settle mostly in major urban areas like Toronto and Vancouver.[189]

In common with many other developed countries, Canada is experiencing a demographic shift towards an older population, with more retirees and fewer people of working age. In 2006, the average age of the population was 39.5 years.[190] The census results also indicate that despite an increase in immigration since 2001 (which gave Canada a higher rate of population growth than in the previous intercensal period), the aging of Canada's population did not slow during the period.

Support for religious pluralism is an important part of Canada's political culture. According to the 2001 census, 77.1% of Canadians identify as being Christians; of this, Catholics make up the largest group (43.6% of Canadians).[187] The largest Protestant denomination is the United Church of Canada (9.5% of Canadians), followed by the Anglicans (6.8%), Baptists (2.4%), Lutherans (2%), and other Christians (4.4%).[187] About 16.5% of Canadians declare no religious affiliation, and the remaining 6.3% are affiliated with non-Christian religions, the largest of which is Islam (2.0%), followed by Judaism (1.1%).[187]

Canadian provinces and territories are responsible for education. Each system is similar, while reflecting regional history, culture and geography.[191] The mandatory school age ranges between 5–7 to 16–18 years,[191] contributing to an adult literacy rate of 99%.[8] Post-secondary education is also administered by provincial and territorial governments, which provide most of the funding; the federal government administers additional research grants, student loans, and scholarships. In 2002, 43% of Canadians aged 25 to 64 possessed a post-secondary education; for those aged 25 to 34, the rate of post-secondary education reached 51%.[192]

Culture

Canadian culture has historically been influenced by British, French, and aboriginal cultures and traditions. There are distinctive Aboriginal cultures, languages, art, and music spread across Canada.[193] [194] Many North American Indigenous words, inventions and games have become an everyday part of Canadian language and use. The canoe, snowshoes, the toboggan, lacrosse, tug of war, maple syrup and tobacco are examples of products, inventions and games.[195] Some of the words include the barbecue, caribou, chipmunk, woodchuck, hammock, skunk, mahogany, hurricane and moose.[196] Numerous areas, towns, cities and rivers of the Americas have names of Indigenous origin. The province of Saskatchewan derives its name from the Cree language name of the Saskatchewan River, "Kisiskatchewani Sipi".[197] Canada's capital city Ottawa comes from

Bill Reid's sculpture *Raven and The First Men*, showing part of a Haida creation myth. The Raven is a figure common to many mythologies in aboriginal culture.

the Algonquin language term "adawe" meaning "to trade."[197] National Aboriginal Day recognises the cultures and contributions of Aboriginal peoples of Canada.[198]

Canadian culture has been greatly influenced by immigration from all over the world. Many Canadians value multiculturalism and see Canada as being inherently multicultural.[69] However, the country's culture has been heavily influenced by American culture because of its proximity and the high rate of migration between the two countries. The great majority of English-speaking immigrants to Canada between 1755 and 1815 were Americans from the Thirteen Colonies; during and immediately after the American Revolutionary War, 46,000 Americans loyal to the British crown came to Canada.[199] Between 1785 and 1812, more Americans emigrated to Canada in response to promises of land.[200]

American media and entertainment are popular, if not dominant, in English Canada; conversely, many Canadian cultural products and entertainers are successful in the United States and worldwide.[201] Many cultural products are marketed toward a unified "North American" or global market. The creation and preservation of distinctly Canadian culture are supported by federal government programs, laws, and institutions such as the Canadian Broadcasting Corporation (CBC), the National Film Board of Canada, and the Canadian Radio-television and Telecommunications Commission.[202]

The Jack Pine, by Tom Thomson, 1916; oil on canvas, in the collection of the National Gallery of Canada

Canadian visual art has been dominated by Tom Thomson — Canada's most famous painter — and by the Group of Seven. Thomson's brief career painting Canadian landscapes spanned just a decade up to his death in 1917 at age 39.[203] The Group were painters with a nationalistic and idealistic focus, who first exhibited their distinctive works in May 1920. Though referred to as having seven members, five artists — Lawren Harris, A. Y. Jackson, Arthur Lismer, J. E. H. MacDonald, and Frederick Varley — were responsible for articulating the Group's ideas. They were joined briefly by Frank Johnston, and by commercial artist Franklin Carmichael. A. J. Casson became part of the Group in 1926.[204] Associated with the Group was another prominent Canadian artist, Emily Carr, known for her landscapes and portrayals of the indigenous peoples of the Pacific Northwest Coast.[205]

Canada has developed a music infrastructure and industry, with broadcasting regulated by the Canadian Radio-television and Telecommunications Commission.[206] [207] The Canadian music industry has produced internationally renowned composers, musicians and ensembles, such as Portia White, Guy Lombardo, Murray Adaskin, Rush, Joni Mitchell and Neil Young. Canadian winners of multiple Grammy Awards have included Celine Dion, k.d. lang, Sarah McLachlan, Alanis Morissette and Shania Twain. The Canadian Academy of Recording Arts and Sciences administers Canada's music industry awards, the Juno Awards, which commenced in 1970.

The national anthem of Canada *O Canada* adopted in 1980, was originally commissioned by the Lieutenant Governor of Quebec, the Honourable Théodore Robitaille, for the 1880 St. Jean-Baptiste Day ceremony.[208] Calixa Lavallée wrote the music, which was a setting of a patriotic poem composed by the poet and judge Sir Adolphe-Basile Routhier. The text was originally only in French, before it was translated to English in 1906.[209]

Canada's National symbols are influenced by natural, historical, and Aboriginal sources. The use of the maple leaf as a Canadian symbol dates to the early 18th century. The maple leaf is depicted on Canada's current and previous flags, on the penny, and on the Coat of Arms.[210] Other prominent symbols include the beaver, Canada Goose, Common Loon, the Crown, the Royal Canadian Mounted Police,[210] and more recently, the totem pole and Inukshuk.[211]

A scene at the 2010 Winter Olympics in Vancouver seconds after Team Canada won gold in men's ice hockey

Canada's official national sports are hockey in the winter and lacrosse in the summer.[212] Hockey is a national pastime and the most popular spectator sport in the country. It is also the sport most played by Canadians, with 1.65 million participants in 2004.[213] Canada's six largest metropolitan areas—Toronto, Montreal, Vancouver, Ottawa, Calgary, and Edmonton—have franchises in the National Hockey League (NHL), and there are more Canadian players in the NHL than from all other countries combined. Other popular spectator sports include curling and football; the latter is played professionally in the Canadian Football League (CFL).[213] Golf, baseball, skiing, soccer, volleyball, and basketball are widely played at youth and amateur levels, but professional leagues and franchises are not widespread.[213]

Canada has hosted several high-profile international sporting events, including the 1976 Summer Olympics in Montreal, the 1988 Winter Olympics in Calgary, and the 2007 FIFA U-20 World Cup. Canada was the host nation for the 2010 Winter Olympics in Vancouver and Whistler, British Columbia.[214]

Language

Canada's two official languages are English and French. Official bilingualism is defined in the Canadian Charter of Rights and Freedoms, the Official Languages Act, and *Official Language Regulations*; it is applied by the Commissioner of Official Languages. English and French have equal status in federal courts, Parliament, and in all federal institutions. Citizens have the right, where there is sufficient demand, to receive federal government services in either English or French, and official-language minorities are guaranteed their own schools in all provinces and territories.[215]

Notre-Dame-des-Victoires in the historic *Basse-Ville* (Lower Town) of Quebec City, Quebec. The population is mainly French-speaking, with a small English-speaking minority.

English and French are the mother tongues of 59.7% and 23.2% of the population respectively,[216] and the languages most spoken at home by 68.3% and 22.3% of the population respectively.[217] 98.5% of Canadians speak English or French (67.5% speak English only, 13.3% speak French only, and 17.7% speak both).[218] English and French Official Language Communities, defined by First Official Language Spoken, constitute 73.0% and 23.6% of the population respectively.[218]

The Charter of the French Language makes French the official language in Quebec.[219] Although more than 85% of French-speaking Canadians live in Quebec, there are substantial Francophone populations in Ontario, Alberta, and southern Manitoba; Ontario has the largest French-speaking population outside Quebec.[220] New Brunswick, the only officially bilingual province, has a French-speaking Acadian minority constituting 33% of the population. There are also clusters of Acadians in southwestern Nova Scotia, on Cape Breton Island, and through central and western Prince Edward Island.[221]

Other provinces have no official languages as such, but French is used as a language of instruction, in courts, and for other government services in addition to English. Manitoba, Ontario, and Quebec allow for both English and French to be spoken in the provincial legislatures, and laws are enacted in both languages. In Ontario, French has some legal status but is not fully co-official.[222] There are 11 Aboriginal language groups, made up of more than 65 distinct dialects.[223] Of these, only Cree, Inuktitut and Ojibway have a large enough population of fluent speakers to be considered viable to survive in the long term.[224] Several aboriginal languages have official status in the Northwest Territories.[225] Inuktitut is the majority language in Nunavut, and one of three official languages in the territory.[226]

Over six million people in Canada list a non-official language as their mother tongue. Some of the most common non-official first languages include Chinese (mainly Cantonese; 1,012,065 first-language speakers), Italian (455,040), German (450,570), Punjabi (367,505) and Spanish (345,345).[216]

International rankings

Organization	Survey	Ranking
State of World Liberty Project	State of World Liberty Index[227]	3 out of 159
United Nations Development Programme	Human Development Index[9]	4 out of 182
World Bank	Ease of Doing Business 2009[228]	8 out of 181
The Economist	The World in 2005 – Worldwide quality-of-life index, 2005[229]	14 out of 111
Yale University/Columbia University	Environmental Sustainability Index, 2005[230]	6 out of 146
Reporters Without Borders	Press Freedom Index 2009[231]	19 out of 175
Transparency International	Corruption Perceptions Index 2009[232]	8 out of 180
Institute for Economics & Peace	Global Peace Index[233]	8 out of 144
Fund for Peace	Failed States Index, 2009[234]	166 out of 177[235]
World Economic Forum	Global Competitiveness Report[236]	9 out of 133
The Economist	Democracy Index[237]	11 out of 167

See also

- Outline of Canada
- Index of Canada-related articles
- Canada-related topics by provinces and territories

Further reading

History

- Bumsted, JM (2004). *History of the Canadian Peoples*. Oxford, UK: Oxford University Press. ISBN 0-19-541688-0.
- Conrad, Margaret; Finkel, Alvin (2003). *Canada: A National History*. Toronto: Longman. ISBN 0-201-73060-X.
- Stewart, Gordon T (1996). *History of Canada Before 1867*. East Lansing, MI: Michigan State University Press. ISBN 0-87013-398-5.

Government and law

- Brooks, Stephen (2000). *Canadian Democracy: An Introduction* (3rd ed.). Don Mills, ON: Oxford University Press Canada. ISBN 0-19-541503-5.
- Dahlitz, Julie (2003). *Secession and international law: conflict avoidance – regional appraisals*. The Hague: T.M.C. Asser Press. ISBN 90-6704-142-4.

Foreign relations and military

- Fox, Annette Baker (1996). *Canada in World Affairs*. East Lansing: Michigan State University Press. ISBN 0-87013-391-8.
- Morton, Desmond; Granatstein, JL (1989). *Marching to Armageddon: Canadians and the Great War 1914–1919*. Toronto: Lester & Orpen Dennys. ISBN 0-88619-209-9.

Geography and climate

- Quentin H. Stanford, ed (2003). *Canadian Oxford World Atlas* (5th ed.). Toronto: Oxford University Press (Canada). ISBN 0-19-541897-2.

Economy

- Marr, William L; Paterson, Donald G (1980). *Canada: An Economic History*. Toronto: Gage. ISBN 0-7715-5684-5.
- Wallace, Iain (2002). *A Geography of the Canadian Economy*. Don Mills, ON: Oxford University Press. ISBN 0-19-540773-3.

Demography and statistics

- Statistics Canada (2001). *Canada Year Book*. Ottawa: Queen of Canada. ISBN 0-660-18360-9.

Language

- "Annual Report – Special Edition" [238]. Office of the Commissioner of Official Languages. 2005. Retrieved 2009-10-19.

Culture

- Resnick, Philip (2005). *The European Roots Of Canadian Identity*. Peterborough, Ont.: Broadview Press. ISBN 1-55111-705-3.

External links

Government

- Official website of the Government of Canada [239]
- Official website of the Governor General of Canada [240]
- Official website of the Prime Minister of Canada [241]

Crown corporations

- Canada Post [242]
- Canadian Broadcasting Corporation [243]

Other

- Canada [244] at *UCB Libraries GovPubs*
- Canada [245] at the Open Directory Project
- Canadian Studies: A Guide to the Sources [246]
- Citizenship and Immigration Canada [247]
- The Dictionary of Canadian Biography [248], – biographies of Canadians from 1000 to 1930 CE.

References

[1] Department of Canadian Heritage. "Ceremonial and Canadian Symbols Promotion > Royal anthem "God Save The Queen"" (http://www. pch.gc.ca/pgm/ceem-cced/symbl/godsave-eng.cfm). Queen's Printer for Canada. . Retrieved 25 June 2010.

[2] Kallmann, Helmut. "The Canadian Encyclopedia" (http://thecanadianencyclopedia.com/index.cfm?PgNm=TCE& Params=U1ARTU0002533). in Marsh, James Harley. *Encyclopedia of Music in Canada > Musical Genres > National and royal anthems.* Toronto: Historica Foundation of Canada. . Retrieved 25 June 2010

[3] "Official Languages Act" (http://www.assembly.gov.nt.ca/_live/documents/documentManagerUpload/08-09-02 Official Languages Act.pdf) (PDF). *Revised Statutes of NWT, 1988.* Department of Justice, Northwest Territories. . Retrieved 2009-11-01.

[4] D'Aquino, Thomas; Doern, G. Bruce; Blair, Cassandra (1983). *Parliamentary democracy in Canada: issues for reform.* ITP Nelson. p. 2. ISBN 0458962902.

[5] "Canada's population clock" (http://www.statcan.gc.ca/pub/82-003-x/pop/pop-h-clock-eng.htm). Statistics Canada. . Retrieved 2010-08-6.

[6] "Ethnic origins, 2006 counts, for Canada, provinces and territories − 20% sample data" (http://www12.statcan.ca/english/census06/data/ highlights/ethnic/pages/Page.cfm?Lang=E&Geo=PR&Code=01&Table=2&Data=Count&StartRec=1&Sort=3&Display=All/). Statistics Canada. 2008-01-04. . Retrieved 2009-10-19.

[7] "Canada" (http://www.imf.org/external/pubs/ft/weo/2010/01/weodata/weorept.aspx?sy=2007&ey=2010&scsm=1&ssd=1& sort=country&ds=.&br=1&c=156&s=NGDPD,NGDPDPC,PPPGDP,PPPPC,LP&grp=0&a=&pr.x=39&pr.y=14). International Monetary Fund. . Retrieved 2010-04-21.

[8] "The World Factbook: Canada" (https://www.cia.gov/library/publications/the-world-factbook/geos/ca.html). Central Intelligence Agency. 2006-05-16. . Retrieved 2009-10-19.

[9] "Human Development Report 2009" (http://hdr.undp.org/en/media/HDR_2009_EN_Complete.pdf). United Nations Development Program. 2009. p. 171. . Retrieved 2010-02-07.

[10] "Territorial evolution" (http://atlas.nrcan.gc.ca/site/english/maps/reference/anniversary_maps/terr_evol) (html/PDF). *Atlas of Canada.* Natural Resources Canada. . Retrieved 2007-10-09.

[11] "Canada: History" (http://www.thecommonwealth.org/YearbookInternal/145152/history/) (html/PDF). *Country Profiles.* Commonwealth Secretariat. . Retrieved 2007-10-09.

[12] "Origin of the Name, Canada" (http://www.pch.gc.ca/pgm/ceem-cced/symbl/o5-eng.cfm). Canadian Heritage (Government of Canada). 2008. . Retrieved 2010-06-27.

[13] Maura, Juan Francisco (2009). "Nuevas aportaciones al estudio de la toponimia ibérica en la América Septentrional en el siglo XVI". *Bulletin of Spanish Studies* (Routledge) **86** (5): 577−603. doi:10.1080/14753820902969345.

[14] Rayburn, Alan (2001). *Naming Canada: Stories of Canadian Place Names* (2nd ed.). Toronto: University of Toronto Press. pp. 1−22. ISBN 0-8020-8293-9.

[15] Clarke, Michael (1998). *Canada: Portraits of the Faith.* Reel to Real. p. 60. ISBN 0968183506.

[16] Phillip Buckner, ed (2008). *Canada and the British Empire.* Oxford University Press. pp. 37−40, 56−59, 114, 124−125. ISBN 019927164X.

[17] "Y-Chromosome Evidence for Differing Ancient Demographic Histories in the Americas" (http://www.ucl.ac.uk/tcga/tcgapdf/ Bortolini-AJHG-03-YAmer.pdf) (PDF). University College London 73:524−539. 2003. doi:10.1086/377588. . Retrieved 2010-01-22.

[18] Cinq-Mars, J (2001). "On the significance of modified mammoth bones from eastern Beringia" (http://web.archive.org/web/*/http:// www.palanth.com/forum/upload_download/articles/cinqmars_elefanti_01.pdf) (PDF). *The World of Elephants − International Congress, Rome.* . Retrieved 2010-02-25.

[19] Wright, JV (2001-09-27). "A History of the Native People of Canada: Early and Middle Archaic Complexes" (http://www.civilization.ca/ cmc/exhibitions/archeo/hnpc/npvol04e.shtml). Canadian Museum of Civilization Corporation. . Retrieved 2009-10-19.

[20] Griebel, Ron. "The Bluefish Caves" (http://www.mnsu.edu/emuseum/archaeology/sites/northamerica/bluefishcaves.html). Minnesota State University. . Retrieved 2009-09-18.

[21] "Beringia: humans were here" (http://www.canada.com/montrealgazette/news/saturdayextra/story. html?id=2a31375e-e834-407d-b8db-2a0010ad4acf&p=2) (re-published online by Canada.com). *Gazette (Montreal).* CanWest MediaWorks Publications Inc.. May 17, 2008. . Retrieved 2009-09-18.

[22] Cinq-Mars, Jacques (2001). "Significance of the Bluefish Caves in Beringian Prehistory" (http://www.civilization.ca/cmc/explore/ resources-for-scholars/essays/archaeology/jacques-cinq-mars/significance-of-the-bluefish-caves-in-beringian-prehistory2#four). Canadian Museum of Civilization. p. 2. . Retrieved 2010-04-15.

[23] Dickason, Olive, ed (1995). *The Native Imprint: The Contribution of First Peoples to Canada's Character.* 1. Athabasca: Athabasca University Educational Enterprises. pp. 114−117.

[24] Peter Turchin, Leonid Grinin, Andrey Korotayev, and Victor C. de Munck., ed (2006). *History & Mathematics: Historical Dynamics and Development of Complex Societies* (http://edurss.ru/cgi-bin/db.pl?cp=&page=Book&id=53185&lang=en&blang=en&list=Found). Moscow: KomKniga/URSS. ISBN 5484010020. .

[25] Wilson, Donna M; Northcott, Herbert C (2008). *Dying and Death in Canada* (http://books.google.com/?id=p_pMVs53mzQC& pg=PA25&dq&q=). Toronto: University of Toronto Press. pp. 25−27. ISBN 9781551118734. . Retrieved 2010-06-20.

[26] Thornton, Russell (2000). "Population history of Native North Americans". in Michael R. Haines, Richard Hall Steckel. *A population history of North America.* Cambridge: Cambridge University Press. p. 13. ISBN 0521496667.

[27] "Handbook of North American Indians: Indians in contemporary society". Garrick Alan Bailey (2008). Government Printing Office. p.285. ISBN 0160803888

[28] "Civilization.ca-Gateway to Aboriginal Heritage-Culture" (http://www.civilization.ca/cmc/exhibitions/tresors/ethno/etb0170e.shtml). Canadian Museum of Civilization Corporation. Government of Canada. May 12, 2006. . Retrieved 2009-09-18.

[29] "Inuit Circumpolar Council (Canada)-ICC Charter" (http://inuitcircumpolar.com/index.php?auto_slide=&ID=374&Lang=En& Parent_ID=&current_slide_num=). Inuit Circumpolar Council > ICC Charter and By-laws > ICC Charter. 2007. . Retrieved 2009-09-18.

[30] "In the Kawaskimhon Aboriginal Moot Court Factum of the Federal Crown Canada" (http://www.umanitoba.ca/law/newsite/ kawaskimhon_factums/FINALWrittenSubmissionsofFederalCrown_windsor.pdf) (PDF). Faculty of Law. University of Manitoba. 2007. p. 2. . Retrieved 2009-09-18.

[31] "What to Search: Topics-Canadian Genealogy Centre-Library and Archives Canada" (http://www.collectionscanada.gc.ca/genealogie/ 022-905.004-e.html). Ethno-Cultural and Aboriginal Groups. Government of Canada. 2009-05-27. . Retrieved 2009-10-02.

[32] "Innu Culture 3. Innu-Inuit 'Warfare'" (http://www.heritage.nf.ca/aboriginal/innu_culture.html). 1999, Adrian Tanner Department of Anthropology-Memorial University of Newfoundland. . Retrieved 2009-10-05.

[33] Pálsson, Hermann (1965) (Digitized online by Google books). The Vinland sagas: the Norse discovery of America (http://books.google. ca/books?id=m-4rb_GhQ5EC&lpg=PP1&dq=The Vinland sagas: the Norse discovery of America&pg=PA28#v=onepage&q&f=true). Penguin Classics. p. 28. ISBN 0140441549. . Retrieved 2010-04-15.

[34] Reeves, Arthur Middleton (2009) (Digitized online by Google books). The Norse Discovery of America (http://books.google.ca/ books?id=HkoPUdPM3V8C&pg=PA7&dq=The+Norse+discoverers+of+America,+the+Wineland+sagas&hl=en& ei=to3HS_vvJoT7lwfnhNHFAQ&sa=X&oi=book_result&ct=result&resnum=6&ved=0CE8Q6AEwBQ#v=onepage&q&f=true). BiblioLife. p. 82. . Retrieved 2010-04-15.

[35] "John Cabot's voyage of 1498" (http://www.heritage.nf.ca/exploration/cabot1498.html). Memorial University of Newfoundland (Newfoundland and Labrador Heritage). 2000. . Retrieved 2010-04-12.

[36] "The Portuguese Explorers" (http://www.heritage.nf.ca/exploration/portuguese.html). Memorial University of Newfoundland. 2004. . Retrieved 2010-06-27.

[37] Morton, Desmond (2001). A Short History of Canada (6th ed.). Toronto: McClelland & Stewart. pp. 9–17. ISBN 0-7710-6509-4.

[38] Morton, Desmond (2001) (pp. 17–19)

[39] Morton, Desmond (2001) (p. 33)

[40] Smith, Philip (April 1987). "Transhuman Europeans Overseas: The Newfoundland Case". Current Anthropology (University of Chicago Press) 28 (2): 241–250. doi:10.1086/203526.

[41] Morton, Desmond (2001) (pp. 89–104)

[42] Sarkonak, Ralph (1983). "A Brief Chronology of French Canada, 1534–1982". Yale French Studies (Yale University Press) (65): 275–282.

[43] Bumsted, JM (1987). Land, settlement, and politics on eighteenth-century Prince Edward Island. McGill-Queen's University Press. p. 30. ISBN 0773505660.

[44] Moore, Christopher (1994). The Loyalist: Revolution Exile Settlement. Toronto: McClelland & Stewart. ISBN 0-7710-6093-9.

[45] McNairn, Jeffrey L (2000). The capacity to judge. Toronto: University of Toronto Press. p. 24. ISBN 0802043607.

[46] This is a photograph taken in 1885 of the now-destroyed 1884 painting.

[47] Haines, Michael; Steckel, Richard Hall (2000). A population history of North America. Cambridge University Press. p. 380. ISBN 9780521496667.

[48] "Immigration History of Canada" (http://faculty.marianopolis.edu/c.belanger/QuebecHistory/encyclopedia/ ImmigrationHistoryofCanada.htm). Marianopolis College. 2004. . Retrieved 2008-01-26.

[49] Romney, Paul (Spring 1989). "From Constitutionalism to Legalism: Trial by Jury, Responsible Government, and the Rule of Law in the Canadian Political Culture". Law and History Review (University of Illinois Press) 7 (1): 128.

[50] Evenden, Leonard J; Turbeville, Daniel E (1992). "The Pacific Coast Borderland and Frontier". in Donald G. Janelle. Geographical snapshots of North America. Guilford Press. p. 52. ISBN 0898620309.

[51] Bothwell, Robert (1996). History of Canada Since 1867. East Lansing, MI: Michigan State University Press. pp. 207–310. ISBN 0-87013-399-3.

[52] Bumsted, JM (1996). The Red River Rebellion. Winnipeg: Watson & Dwyer. ISBN 0920486231.

[53] "Building a nation" (http://www.canadiangeographic.ca/Atlas/themes.aspx?id=building&sub=building_basics_confederation& lang=En). The Canadian Atlas. . Retrieved 2009-09-18.

[54] Bothwell, Robert (1996) (p. 31).

[55] "Sir John A. Macdonald" (http://www.collectionscanada.gc.ca/sir-john-a-macdonald/023013-5000-e.html). Library and Archives Canada. 2008. . Retrieved 2009-09-18.

[56] Cook, Terry (2000). "The Canadian West: An Archival Odyssey through the Records of the Department of the Interior" (http://www. collectionscanada.gc.ca/publications/archivist-magazine/015002-2230-e.html). The Archivist. Library and Archives Canada. . Retrieved 2009-09-18.

[57] Morton, Desmond (1999). A military history of Canada (4th ed.). Toronto: McClelland & Stewart. pp. 130–158, 173, 203–233. ISBN 0771065140.

[58] Haglund, David G; MacFarlane, S Neil (1999). Security, strategy and the global economics of defence production. McGill-Queen's University Press. p. 12. ISBN 0889118752.

[59] Dellinger, Walter (Autumn 1982). "The Amending Process in Canada and the United States: A Comparative Perspective". *Law & Contemporary Problems* (Duke Law School) **45** (4): 291.

[60] Young, Walter (1983). "Canada: The Social Democracy of Provincial Government in a Federal System". in Peter Davis. *Social Democracy in the South Pacific*. **2**. Auckland, New Zealand: Ross. pp. 48–58. ISBN 0908636350.

[61] Goddard, Lance (2005). *Canada and the Liberation of the Netherlands*. Dundurn Press Ltd. pp. 225–232. ISBN 1550025473.

[62] Stacey, CP (1948). *History of the Canadian Army in the Second World War*. **1**. Queen's Printer. pp. 324–327.

[63] Sherwood, George; Sherwood, Stewart (2006). *Legends in their time*. Natural Heritage Books. p. 162. ISBN 1897045107.

[64] "Dominion of Newfoundland" (http://fcinternet.hwdsb.on.ca/~nathan.tidridge/S010EAA85.48/Dominion of Newfoundland.pdf) (PDF). Hamilton-Wentworth District School Board. 1999. . Retrieved 2010-06-07.

[65] Mackey, Eva (2002). *The house of difference: cultural politics and national identity in Canada*. Toronto: University of Toronto Press. p. 57. ISBN 0802084818.

[66] Esman, Milton J (Summer 1982). "The Politics of Official Bilingualism in Canada" (http://jstor.org/stable/2149477). *Political Science Quarterly* (The Academy of Political Science) **97** (2): 233–253. doi:10.2307/2149477. .

[67] Esses, Victoria M; Gardner, RC (July 1996). "Multiculturalism in Canada: Context and current status". *Canadian Journal of Behavioural Science* (American Psychological Association) **28** (3): 145–152.

[68] Sarrouh, Elissar (2002-01-22). "Social Policies in Canada: A Model for Development" (http://www.escwa.un.org/information/publications/edit/upload/sd-01-09.pdf). *Social Policy Series, No. 1*. United Nations. pp. 14–16, 22–37. . Retrieved 2010-01-17.

[69] Bickerton, James; Gagnon, Alain, eds (2004). *Canadian Politics* (4th ed.). Orchard Park, NY: Broadview Press. pp. 250–254, 344–347. ISBN 1-55111-595-6.

[70] Légaré, André (2008). "Canada's Experiment with Aboriginal Self-Determination in Nunavut: From Vision to Illusion". *International Journal on Minority and Group Rights* (Martinus Nijhoff Publishers) **15** (2–3): 335–367. doi:10.1163/157181108X332659.

[71] Tonelli, Carla (July–August 2007). "Oka, 1990: "Our land is our future"" (http://www.thismagazine.ca/issues/2007/07/risingup.php#oka). This Magazine. . Retrieved 2008-05-29. "The most memorable photos come from this period, including the nose-to-nose standoff between Private Patrick Cloutier and Brad 'Freddy Krueger' Larocque, often misidentified as Ronald 'Lasagna' Cross."

[72] Clift, Dominique (1982). *Quebec nationalism in crisis* (reissued ed.). McGill-Queen's University Press. pp. 28–36, 96–99, 106–107. ISBN 0773503838.

[73] Dickinson, John Alexander; Young, Brian (2003). *A Short History of Quebec* (3rd ed.). Montreal: McGill-Queen's University Press. pp. 357–360. ISBN 0-7735-2450-9.

[74] "Commission of Inquiry into the Investigation of the Bombing of Air India Flight 182" (http://www.majorcomm.ca/en/termsofreference/). Canadian government. . Retrieved 2009-06-01.

[75] Sourour, Teresa K (1991). "Report of Coroner's Investigation" (http://www.diarmani.com/Montreal_Coroners_Report.pdf) (PDF). . Retrieved 2010-06-07.

[76] "The Oka Crisis" (http://archives.cbc.ca/politics/civil_unrest/topics/99/) (Digital Archives). Canadian Broadcasting Corporation. 2000. . Retrieved 2010-06-07.

[77] Roach, Kent (2003). *September 11: consequences for Canada*. McGill-Queen's University Press. pp. 15, 59–61, 194.

[78] "Canada and Multilateral Operations in Support of Peace and Stability" (http://www.forces.gc.ca/site/news-nouvelles/news-nouvelles-eng.asp?cat=00&id=914). National Defence and the Canadian Forces. 2010. . Retrieved 2010-06-07.

[79] Jockel, Joseph T; Sokolsky, Joel B (2008). "Canada and the war in Afghanistan: NATO's odd man out steps forward". *Journal of Transatlantic Studies* (Routledge) **6** (1): 100–115. doi:10.1080/14794010801917212.

[80] Victoria (March 29, 1867). *Constitution Act, 1867* (http://www.solon.org/Constitutions/Canada/English/ca_1867.html). III.15. Westminster: Queen's Printer. . Retrieved January 15, 2009

[81] Smith, David E. (10 June 2010). "The Crown and the Constitution: Sustaining Democracy?" (http://www.queensu.ca/iigr/conf/ConferenceOnTheCrown/CrownConferencePapers/The_Crown_and_the_Constitutio1.pdf). *The Crown in Canada: Present Realities and Future Options* (Kingston: Queen's University): p. 6. . Retrieved 18 May 2010

[82] Department of Canadian Heritage (February 2009). *Canadian Heritage Portfolio* (http://www.pch.gc.ca/pc-ch/publctn/gp-pg/ppc-chp/ppc-chp-eng.pdf) (2 ed.). Ottawa: Queen's Printer for Canada. pp. 3–4. ISBN 978-1-100-11529-0. . Retrieved July 5, 2009

[83] MacLeod, Kevin S. (2008). *A Crown of Maples* (http://www.pch.gc.ca/pgm/ceem-cced/fr-rf/crnCdn/crn_mpls-eng.pdf) (1 ed.). Ottawa: Queen's Printer for Canada. p. 16. ISBN 978-0-662-46012-1. . Retrieved June 21, 2009

[84] Jean, Michaëlle (November 2005). "Canada: terre de liberté et d'aventures" (in French). *Policy Options* (Institute for Research on Public Policy) **26** (9): 5–6.

[85] *Commonwealth public administration reform 2004*. Commonwealth Secretariat. 2004. pp. 54–55. ISBN 0117032492.

[86] Forsey 2005, p. 1

[87] Marleau, Robert; Montpetit, Camille. "House of Commons Procedure and Practice > 1. Parliamentary Institutions" (http://www2.parl.gc.ca/MarleauMontpetit/DocumentViewer.aspx?DocId=1001&Sec=Ch01&Seq=5&Lang=E&Print=2). Queen's Printer for Canada. . Retrieved September 28, 2009.

[88] Russell, Peter (1983). "Bold Statecraft, Questionable Jurisprudence" (http://books.google.com/?id=sUwOAAAAQAAJ&printsec=frontcover&q). in Banting, Keith G.; Simeon, Richard. *And no one cheered: federalism, democracy, and the Constitution Act*. Toronto: Taylor & Francis. p. 217. ISBN 9780458959501. . Retrieved 12 June 2010

[89] "Prime Minister of Canada" (http://www.pm.gc.ca/eng/pm.asp?featureId=7). Queen's Printer for Canada. 2009. . Retrieved October 23, 2003.

[90] Johnson, David (2006). *Thinking government: public sector management in Canada* (2nd ed.). Toronto: University of Toronto Press. pp. 134–135, 149. ISBN 1551117797.

[91] Forsey 2005, p. 16

[92] Liberal Party of Canada (2009). "Michael Ignatieff" (http://www.liberal.ca/en/michael-ignatieff/biography). Federal Liberal Agency of Canada. . Retrieved October 23, 2008.

[93] Dawson, R. MacGregor; Dawson, WF (1989). Norman Ward. ed. *Democratic Government in Canada*. Toronto: University of Toronto Press. pp. 16–17, 59–60, 66. ISBN 0802067034.

[94] Hicks, Bruce M.; Blais, André (2008). "Restructuring the Canadian Senate through Elections". *IIRP Choices* (Institute for Research on Public Policy) **14** (14): 11.

[95] Stevenson, Garth (2004). *Unfulfilled union: Canadian federalism and national unity* (4th ed.). McGill-Queen's University Press. p. 30. ISBN 0773527443.

[96] Intergovernmental Affairs Canada (2009). "Difference between Canadian Provinces and Territories" (http://www.pco-bcp.gc.ca/aia/ index.asp?lang=eng&page=provterr&sub=difference&doc=difference-eng.htm). Queen's Printer for Canada. . Retrieved September 19, 2009.

[97] Legislative Assembly of the Northwest Territories (2008). "A Comparison of Provincial & Territorial Governments" (http://www. assembly.gov.nt.ca/_live/pages/wpPages/factscomparisonofprovincialandterritorial.aspx). Queen's Printer for Canada. . Retrieved March 10, 2010.

[98] Legislative Assembly of Nunavut (2008). "Frequently Asked Questions" (http://www.assembly.nu.ca/english/about/FAQ.htm#18). Queen's Printer for Canada. . Retrieved September 19, 2009.

[99] Bakan, Joel; Elliot, Robin M (2003). *Canadian Constitutional Law*. Emond Montgomery Publications. pp. 3–8, 683–687, 699. ISBN 1552390853.

[100] The Constitution Act, 1867 (U.K.), 30 & 31 Victoria, c. 3.

[101] "Canadian Culture And Ethnic Diversity" (http://www.multiculturalcanada.ca/Encyclopedia/A-Z/c2). Canadian Heritage (Multicultural Canada). 2009-01. . Retrieved 2006-11-30.

[102] Assembly of First Nations; Elizabeth II (2004). "A First Nations – Federal Crown Political Accord" (http://www.afn.ca/cmslib/general/ PolAcc.pdf). 1. Ottawa: Assembly of First Nations. p. 3. . Retrieved 2009-11-17

[103] "Treaty areas" (http://dsp-psd.communication.gc.ca/Collection-R/LoPBdP/EB/prb9916-e.htm). *Treasury Board of Canada Secretariat*. Government of Canada. 2002-10-07. . Retrieved 2009-10-02.

[104] "What is Treaty 8?" (http://www.cbc.ca/news/background/aboriginals/treaty8.html). *Canadian Broadcasting Corporation*. . Retrieved 2009-10-05.

[105] McCormick, Peter (2000). *Supreme at last: the evolution of the Supreme Court of Canada*. James Lorimer & Company Ltd. pp. 2, 86, 154. ISBN 1550286927.

[106] "About the Court" (http://www.scc-csc.gc.ca/court-cour/sys/index-eng.asp). Supreme Court of Canada. 2009. . Retrieved 2009-09-20.

[107] Sworden, Philip James (2006). *An introduction to Canadian law*. Emond Montgomery Publications. pp. 22, 150. ISBN 1552391450.

[108] "Keeping Canada and Our Communities Safe and Secure" (http://www.nbpei-ecn.ca/documents/ECN-Forensics.pdf#neighbourhood). RCMP. . Retrieved 2009-09-20.

[109] Haglung, David G (Autumn 2003). "North American Cooperation in an Era of Homeland Security". *Orbis* (Foreign Policy Research Institute) **47** (4): 675–691. doi:10.1016/S0030-4387(03)00072-3.

[110] James, Patrick (2006). Nelson Michaud, Marc J. O'Reilly. ed. *Handbook of Canadian Foreign Policy*. Lexington Books. pp. 213–214, 349–362. ISBN 073911493X.

[111] "About the Canadian Forces" (http://www.forces.gc.ca/site/acf-apfc/index-eng.asp). Department of National Defence. . Retrieved 2009-12-04.

[112] "Defence Minister Welcomes Auditor General's Reportpublisher=DND" (http://www.forces.gc.ca/site/news-nouvelles/ news-nouvelles-eng.asp?cat=00&id=900). . Retrieved April 25, 1998.

[113] "Canada's equipment in Afghanistan Reportpublisher=CBC" (http://www.cbc.ca/canada/story/2009/07/08/ f-canada-military-land-vehicles.html). . Retrieved July 9, 2009.

[114] "Fleet at a Glance Reportpublisher=DND" (http://www.navy.forces.gc.ca/cms/1/1_eng.asp). . Retrieved 2010-05-10.

[115] "Who We Are – General Information Reportpublisher=DND" (http://www.airforce.forces.gc.ca/v2/page-eng.asp?id=26). . Retrieved 2010-01-14.

[116] Eayrs, James (1980). *In Defence of Canada*. Toronto: University of Toronto Press. p. 332. ISBN 0-8020-2345-2.

[117] *Canada's international policy statement: a role of pride and influence in the world* (http://geo.international.gc.ca/cip-pic/ current_discussions/ips-archive-en.aspx). Ottawa: Government of Canada. 2005. ISBN 0-662-68608-X. . Retrieved 2010-01-19.

[118] Finkel, Alvin (1997). *Our lives: Canada after 1945*. Lorimer. pp. 105–107, 111–116. ISBN 1550285513.

[119] Holloway, Steven Kendall (2006). *Canadian foreign policy: defining the national interest*. Toronto: University of Toronto Press. pp. 102–103. ISBN 1551118165.

[120] Morton, Desmond (1999) (p. 258)

[121] Farnsworth, Clyde H (1994-11-27). "Torture by Army Peacekeepers in Somalia Shocks Canada" (http://www.nytimes.com/1994/11/27/world/torture-by-army-peacekeepers-in-somalia-shocks-canada.html). New York Times. . Retrieved 2010-04-15.

[122] "UN Peacekeeping Current Operations" (http://www.unac.org/peacekeeping/en/un-peacekeeping/current-operations/). United Nations Association Canada. . Retrieved 2009-10-15.

[123] "The UN and peacekeeping" (http://www.unac.org/en/link_learn/fact_sheets/peacekeeping.asp). United Nations Association Canada. . Retrieved 2009-10-15.

[124] "Canada and the Organization of American States (OAS)" (http://www.pch.gc.ca/pgm/ai-ia/rir-iro/am-as/oea-oas-eng.cfm). Canadian Heritage. 2008. . Retrieved 2009-09-20.

[125] "Opening Doors to Asia" (http://www.international.gc.ca/trade-agreements-accords-commerciaux/cimar-rcami/2009/06_apec.aspx). Foreign Affairs and International Trade Canada. 2009. . Retrieved 2009-09-20.

[126] Freeze, Colin (2009-05-29). "A question of protection in Afghanistan" (http://www.theglobeandmail.com/news/world/a-question-of-protection-in-afghanistan/article1156778/). Globe and Mail. . Retrieved 2009-06-20. Registration required

[127] "Cost of the Afghanistan mission 2001–2011" (http://www.afghanconflictmonitor.org/2009/02/canadian-afghan-mission-costs-113billion.html). *Canada's Engagement in Afghanistan*. Government of Canada. 2009-02-25. . Retrieved 2009-05-13.

[128] Konrad, Victor; Nicol, Heather N (2008). *Beyond walls: re-inventing the Canada-United States borderlands*. Ashgate Publishing. pp. 189, 196. ISBN 0754672026.

[129] Vagnoni, Giselda (2007-02-06). "Rich nations to sign $1.5 bln vaccine pact in Italy" (http://www.reuters.com/article/idUSL06661675._CH_.2400). Reuters. . Retrieved 2010-01-18.

[130] Blomfield, Adrian (2007-08-03). "Russia claims North Pole with Arctic flag stunt" (http://www.telegraph.co.uk/news/worldnews/1559165/Russia-claims-North-Pole-with-Arctic-flag-stunt.html). Telegraph. . Retrieved 2009-10-19.

[131] Bird, Richard M (2008-10-22). "Government Finance" (http://www.statcan.gc.ca/pub/11-516-x/sectionh/4057752-eng.htm). *Historical Statistics of Canada*. Statistics Canada. . Retrieved 2010-03-17.

[132] "The World Factbook" (https://www.cia.gov/library/publications/the-world-factbook/). Central Intelligence Agency. 2006-05-16. . Retrieved 2010-03-09.

[133] "Territorial Evolution, 1927" (http://atlas.nrcan.gc.ca/site/english/maps/historical/territorialevolution/1927/1). National Resources Canada. 2004-04-06. . Retrieved 2006-05-14.

[134] Susic, Stela (2006-08-15). "Air Force becomes command authority for CFS Alert" (http://www.forces.gc.ca/site/Commun/ml-fe/article-eng.asp?id=5317). *The Maple Leaf* (National Defence Canada) **12** (17). . Retrieved 2006-10-03.

[135] "Population Density, 2001" (http://atlas.nrcan.gc.ca/site/english/maps/peopleandsociety/population/population2001/density2001). *The Atlas of Canada*. Natural Resources Canada. 2005-06-15. . Retrieved 2010-01-18.

[136] "Significant Canadian Facts" (http://atlas.nrcan.gc.ca/site/english/learningresources/facts/supergeneral.html). Natural Resources Canada. 2004-04-05. . Retrieved 2006-05-16.

[137] *National Atlas of Canada*. Ottawa: Natural Resources Canada. 2005. p. 1. ISBN 0-7705-1198-8.

[138] Pearce, EA; Smith, CG (1984). *The Times Books world weather guide: a city-by-city guide*. New York Times Books. p. 116. ISBN 0812911237.

[139] Bailey, William G; Oke, TR; Rouse, Wayne R (1997). *The surface climates of Canada*. McGill-Queen's University Press. p. 124. ISBN 0773516727.

[140] The Weather Network. "Statistics, Regina SK" (http://web.archive.org/web/20080404034124rn_1/www.theweathernetwork.com/statistics/C02072/CASK0261?CASK0261). Internet Archive. . Retrieved 2010-01-18.

[141] "Canadian Climate Normals or Averages 1971–2000" (http://climate.weatheroffice.gc.ca/climate_normals/index_e.html). Environment Canada. 2004-02-25. . Retrieved 2010-01-18.

[142] Etkin, David; Haque, CE; Brooks, Gregory R (2003-04-30). *An Assessment of Natural Hazards and Disasters in Canada* (http://books.google.com/?id=kaJz_SNNuKMC&pg=PA569&lpg=PA569&dq=wells+"gray+clearwater"+volcanic+field+earthquakes). Springer. pp. 569, 582, 583. ISBN 978-1402011795. .

[143] "Tseax Cone" (http://gsc.nrcan.gc.ca/volcanoes/cat/volcano_e.php?id=svb_tsx_107). *Catalogue of Canadian volcanoes*. Geological Survey of Canada. 2005-08-19. . Retrieved 2008-07-29.

[144] "Gross domestic expenditures on research and development" (http://www.statcan.gc.ca/pub/88-221-x/2008002/part-partie1-eng.htm). Statistics Canada. . Retrieved 2009-01-22.

[145] "Nobel Prize Winners Canada" (http://www.altiusdirectory.com/Society/nobel-prize-winners-canada.html). Altius Directory. . Retrieved 2010-01-18.

[146] "Internet Usage and Population in North America" (http://www.internetworldstats.com/stats14.htm#north). Internet world stats. . Retrieved 2009-08-18.

[147] "DRDC history" (http://www.drdc-rddc.gc.ca/about-apropos/history-histoire-eng.asp). Drdc-rddc.gc.ca. 2009-03-12. . Retrieved 2010-06-06.

[148] Bomb sniffer "Bomb Sniffers Battle Terrorist Threats" (http://www.nrc-cnrc.gc.ca/eng/research/discoveries/safety-security/bomb-sniffers.html). National Research Council Canada. 2010. Bomb sniffer. Retrieved 2010-06-06.

[149] "ACTIVE PHASED ARRAY RADAR (APAR)" (http://www.thales-systems.ca/projects/apar/apar.pdf). Thales-systems Canada. . Retrieved 2005-02-12.

[150] "Top countries in space sciences" (http://www.timeshighereducation.co.uk/story.asp?sectioncode=26&storycode=408577&c=1). Thomson Reuters Agency. . Retrieved 2009-10-08.

[151] "The Canadian Aerospace Industry praises the federal government for recognizing Space as a strategic capability for Canada" (http:// www.newswire.ca/en/releases/archive/March2010/11/c9200.html). newswire. . Retrieved 2010-03-11.

[152] "Black Brant Sounding Rockets" (http://www.bristol.ca/BlackBrant.html). Magellan Aerospace. . Retrieved 2008-03-11.

[153] "Canada on Mars?" (http://www.marketwire.com/press-release/Canada-on-Mars-1022306.htm). marketwire. . Retrieved 2009-07-27.

[154] "Latest release" (http://www.wto.org/english/news_e/pres08_e/pr520_e.htm). World Trade Organization. 2008-04-17. . Retrieved 2008-07-03.

[155] "Index of Economic Freedom" (http://www.heritage.org/Index/). The Heritage Foundation and the Wall Street Journal. 2009. . Retrieved 2009-01-09.

[156] "Imports, exports and trade balance of goods on a balance-of-payments basis, by country or country grouping" (http://www40.statcan.gc. ca/l01/cst01/gblec02a-eng.htm). Statistics Canada. 2009-11-16. . Retrieved 2010-01-17.

[157] " Canada has first yearly trade deficit since 1975 (http://www.theglobeandmail.com/report-on-business/economy/ canada-has-first-yearly-trade-deficit-since-1975/article1462607/)". The Globe and Mail. February 10, 2010.

[158] "Latest release from Labour Force Survey" (http://www.statcan.gc.ca/subjects-sujets/labour-travail/lfs-epa/lfs-epa-eng.htm). Statistics Canada. 2009-11-06. . Retrieved 2009-11-18.

[159] " Budget fights deficit with freeze on future spending (http://toronto.ctv.ca/servlet/an/local/CTVNews/20100304/ budget_2010_100304/20100304?hub=TorontoNewHome)". CTV News. March 4 2010.

[160] " Canada's foreign debt climbs $41-billion (http://www.financialpost.com/news/Canada+foreign+debt+climbs+billion/3165637/ story.html)". Financial Post. June 17, 2010.

[161] " Why foreign investors can't get enough of our debt (http://www.financialpost.com/related/topics/story.html?id=2456708)". Financial Post. January 17, 2010.

[162] " Canada budget tackles deficit, averts election (http://ca.reuters.com/article/domesticNews/idCATRE6234HN20100304)". Reuters. March 4, 2010.

[163] "Employment by Industry" (http://www40.statcan.gc.ca/l01/cst01/econ40-eng.htm). Statistics Canada. 2009-01-08. . Retrieved 2009-10-19.

[164] Easterbrook, WT (March 1995). "Recent Contributions to Economic History: Canada". *Journal of Economic History* (Economic History Society) **19**: 98.

[165] Brown, Charles E (2002). *World energy resources.* Springer. pp. 323, 378–389. ISBN 3540426345.

[166] Clarke, Tony; Campbell, Bruce; Laxer, Gordon (2006-03-10). "US oil addiction could make us sick" (http://parklandinstitute.ca/ downloads/reports/FuellingFortressAmericareport.pdf). Parkland Institute. . Retrieved 2006-05-18.

[167] Britton, John NH (1996). *Canada and the Global Economy: The Geography of Structural and Technological Change.* McGill-Queen's University Press. pp. 26–27, 155–163. ISBN 0773513566.

[168] Leacy, FH (ed.) (1983). "Vl-12" (http://www.statcan.gc.ca/pub/11-516-x/sectionv/4057758-eng.htm#V332_350). Statistics Canada. . Retrieved 2010-01-18.

[169] Granatstein, JL (1997). *Yankee Go Home: Canadians and Anti-Americanism.* Toronto: HarperCollins. ISBN 0-00-638541-9.

[170] Morck, Randall; Tian, Gloria; Yeung, Bernard (2005). "Who owns whom? Economic nationalism and family controlled pyramidal groups in Canada". in Lorraine Eden, Wendy Dobson. *Governance, multinationals, and growth.* Edward Elgar Publishing. p. 50. ISBN 1843769093.

[171] Jenkins, Barbara L (1992). *The paradox of continental production.* Cornell University Press. p. 117. ISBN 0801426766.

[172] "Jean Chrétien" (http://www.cbc.ca/canada/story/2009/07/13/f-jean-chretien.html). CBC. 2009-07-13. . Retrieved 2009-10-20.

[173] Sturgeon, Jamie (2009-03-13). "Jobless rate to peak at 10%: TD" (http://www.nationalpost.com/related/topics/story. html?id=1383376). National Post. . Retrieved 2009-10-20.

[174] Beauchesne, Eric (2007-03-13). "We are 31,612,897" (http://www.canada.com/nationalpost/financialpost/story. html?id=73b94aac-08f0-477f-a72a-b8b640f6658f&k=90795). National Post. . Retrieved 2007-03-13.

[175] Custred, Glynn (2008). "Security Threats on America's Borders". in Alexander Moens. *Immigration policy and the terrorist threat in Canada and the United States.* Fraser Institute. p. 96. ISBN 0889752354.

[176] "Urban-rural population as a proportion of total population, Canada, provinces, territories and health regions" (http://www.statcan.gc.ca/ pub/82-221-x/00503/t/th/4062283-eng.htm). Statistics Canada. 2001. . Retrieved 2009-04-23.

[177] "Estimated population of Canada, 1605 to present" (http://www.statcan.gc.ca/pub/98-187-x/4151287-eng.htm). Statistics Canada. 2009. . Retrieved 2010-04-16.

[178] "Population by selected ethnic origins, by province and territory (2006 Census) (Canada)" (http://www40.statcan.gc.ca/l01/cst01/ demo26a-eng.htm). Statistics Canada. 2009-07-28. . Retrieved 2010-01-19.

[179] "Aboriginal Identity (8), Sex (3) and Age Groups (12) for the Population of Canada, Provinces, Territories, Census Metropolitan Areas and Census Agglomerations, 2006 Census – 20% Sample Data" (http://www12.statcan.ca/english/census06/data/topics/ RetrieveProductTable.cfm?ALEVEL=3&APATH=3&CATNO=&DETAIL=0&DIM=&DS=99&FL=0&FREE=0&GAL=0&GC=99& GK=NA&GRP=1&IPS=&METH=0&ORDER=1&PID=89122&PTYPE=88971&RL=0&S=1&ShowAll=No&StartRow=1&SUB=0& Temporal=2006&Theme=73&VID=0&VNAMEE=&VNAMEF=&GID=837928). *Census > 2006 Census: Data products > Topic-based tabulations >*. Statistics Canada, Government of Canada. 2008-06-12. . Retrieved 2009-09-18.

[180] "One in 6 Canadians is a visible minority" (http://www.cbc.ca/canada/story/2008/04/02/stats-immigration.html). CBC. 2008-04-02. . Retrieved 2009-10-20.

[181] "2006 Census: Ethnic origin, visible minorities, place of work and mode of transportation" (http://www.statcan.gc.ca/daily-quotidien/080402/dq080402a-eng.htm). *The Daily*. Statistics Canada. 2008-04-02. . Retrieved 2010-01-19.

[182] Pendakur, Krishna. "Visible Minorities and Aboriginal Peoples in Vancouver's Labour Market" (http://www.hrsdc.gc.ca/eng/lp/lo/lswe/we/special_projects/RacismFreeInitiative/Pendakur.shtml). Simon Fraser University. . Retrieved 2010-01-18.

[183] "Vancouver" (http://www12.statcan.ca/census-recensement/2006/dp-pd/prof/92-591/Details/Page.cfm?Lang=E&Geo1=CSD&Code1=5915022&Geo2=PR&Code2=59&Data=Count&SearchText=Vancouver&SearchType=Begins&SearchPR=01&B1=All&GeoLevel=&GeoCode=5915022). Statistics Canada. 2009-07-24. . Retrieved 2009-10-20.

[184] "Toronto" (http://www12.statcan.ca/census-recensement/2006/dp-pd/prof/92-591/Details/Page.cfm?Lang=E&Geo1=CSD&Code1=3520005&Geo2=PR&Code2=35&Data=Count&SearchText=Toronto&SearchType=Begins&SearchPR=01&B1=All&GeoLevel=&GeoCode=3520005). Statistics Canada. 2009-07-24. . Retrieved 2009-10-20.

[185] "The Daily, Tuesday, December 4, 2007. 2006 Census: Immigration, citizenship, language, mobility and migration" (http://www.statcan.gc.ca/daily-quotidien/071204/dq071204a-eng.htm). Statistics Canada. 2007-12-04. . Retrieved 2009-10-19.

[186] " The changing face of Canada: booming minority populations by 2031 (http://www.theglobeandmail.com/news/national/the-changing-face-of-canada-booming-minority-populations-by-2031/article1494651/)". The Globe and Mail. March 9, 2010.

[187] "Population by religion, by province and territory (2001 Census)" (http://www40.statcan.gc.ca/l01/cst01/demo30a-eng.htm). Statistics Canada. 2005-01-25. . Retrieved 2010-01-19.

[188] "Government of Canada Tables 2010 Immigration Plan" (http://news.gc.ca/web/article-eng.do?m=/index&nid=492939). Canada News Centre. . Retrieved 2010-01-24.

[189] "When immigration goes awry" (http://www.thestar.com/Canada2020/article/106702). Toronto Star. 2006-07-14. . Retrieved 2010-01-08.

[190] Martel, Laurent; Malenfant, Éric Caron (2009-09-22). "2006 Census: Portrait of the Canadian Population in 2006, by Age and Sex" (http://www12.statcan.ca/census-recensement/2006/as-sa/97-551/index-eng.cfm?CFID=3347169&CFTOKEN=19485112). Statistics Canada. . Retrieved 2009-10-18.

[191] "Overview of Education in Canada" (http://www.educationau-incanada.ca/index.aspx?action=educationsystem-systemeeducation&lang=eng). Council of Ministers of Education, Canada. . Retrieved 2009-10-20.

[192] "Creating Opportunities for All Canadians" (http://www.fin.gc.ca/ec2005/agenda/agc4-eng.asp). Department of Finance Canada. 2005-11-14. . Retrieved 2006-05-22.

[193] "Assembly of First Nations - Assembly of First Nations-The Story" (http://www.afn.ca/article.asp?id=59). Assembly of First Nations. . Retrieved 2009-10-02.

[194] "Civilization.ca-Gateway to Aboriginal Heritage-object" (http://www.civilization.ca/cmc/exhibitions/tresors/ethno/etb0000e.shtml). Canadian Museum of Civilization Corporation. May 12, 2006. . Retrieved 2009-10-02.

[195] "Diverse Peoples – Aboriginal Contributions and Inventions" (http://www.edu.gov.mb.ca/k12/cur/socstud/foundation_gr2/blms/2-2-1c.pdf) (PDF). *The Government of Manitoba*. . Retrieved 2009-10-17.

[196] Newhouse, David. "Hidden in Plain Sight Aboriginal Contributions to Canada and Canadian Identity Creating a new Indian Problem" (http://www.cst.ed.ac.uk/2005conference/papers/Newhouse_paper.pdf) (PDF). *Centre of Canadian Studies, University of Edinburgh*. . Retrieved 2009-10-17.

[197] "Aboriginal place names contribute to a rich tapestry" (http://www.ainc-inac.gc.ca/ai/mr/is/info106-eng.asp). *Indian and Northern Affairs Canada*. . Retrieved 2009-10-17.

[198] "National Aboriginal Day History" (http://dsp-psd.pwgsc.gc.ca/Collection/R32-179-2000E.pdf) (PDF). *Indian and Northern Affairs Canada*. . Retrieved 2009-10-18.

[199] Will Kaufman, Heidi Slettedahl MacPherson, ed (2005). "Settlement Policies". *Britain and the Americas: culture, politics, and history*. ABC-CLIO. p. 888. ISBN 1851094318.

[200] Dollinger, Stefan (2008). *New-dialect formation in Canada: evidence from the English modal auxiliaries*. John Benjamins. p. 66. ISBN 9027231087.

[201] Blackwell, John D (2005). "Culture High and Low" (http://www.iccs-ciec.ca/blackwell.html#culture). International Council for Canadian Studies World Wide Web Service. . Retrieved 2006-03-15.

[202] "Mandate of the National Film Board" (http://www.onf.ca/medias/download/documents/pdf/NFB_STRATEGIC_PLAN.pdf) (PDF). National Film Board of Canada. 2005. . Retrieved 2009-10-20.

[203] Silcox, David P. (1977). "Tom Thomson's life". in Harold Town and David P. Silcox. *Tom Thomson: the silence and the storm*. Toronto: McClelland & Stewart. pp. 49–59. ISBN 077108482X.

[204] Hill, Charles C. (1995). *The Group of Seven – Art for a Nation*. Ottawa: National Gallery of Canada. pp. 15–21, 195. ISBN 077106716X.

[205] Newlands, Anne (1996). *Emily Carr*. Willowdale, Ontario: Firefly Books. pp. 8–9. ISBN 1552090469.

[206] Carl Morey (1997) (Google books). *Music in Canada: A Research and Information Guide* (http://books.google.com/?id=eZQch8ieRtsC&pg=PP1&dq=Music+in+Canada:+A+Research+and+Information+Guide,&q=). New York Garland Publishing. p. 223. ISBN 9780815316039. . Retrieved 2009-10-28.

[207] The Canadian Communications Foundation. "The history of broadcasting in Canada" (http://www.broadcasting-history.ca/timeline/CCFTimeline.html). . Retrieved 2009-10-28.

[208] "'O Canada'" (http://www.thecanadianencyclopedia.com/index.cfm?PgNm=TCE&Params=U1ARTU0002611). The Canadian Encyclopedia. . Retrieved 2009-10-28.

[209] Government of Canada (2008-06-23). "Hymne national du Canada" (http://www.pch.gc.ca/pgm/ceem-cced/symbl/anthem-fra.cfm). *Canadian Heritage*. Government of Canada. . Retrieved 2008-06-26.

[210] Canadian Heritage (2002). *Symbols of Canada*. Ottawa, ON: Canadian Government Publishing. ISBN 0-660-18615-2.

[211] Ruhl, Jeffrey (January 2008). "Inukshuk Rising". *Canadian Journal of Globalization* (CJOG) **1** (1): 25–30.

[212] Wieting, Stephen G (2001). *Sport and memory in North America*. Frank Cass. p. 4. ISBN 0714682055.

[213] Conference Board of Canada (December 2004). "Survey: Most Popular Sports, by Type of Participation, Adult Population" (http://www. pch.gc.ca/progs/sc/pubs/socio-eco/tab2_tab_e.cfm). *Strengthening Canada: The Socio-economic Benefits of Sport Participation in Canada—Report August 2005*. Sport Canada. . Retrieved 2006-07-01.

[214] "Vancouver 2010" (http://www.vancouver2010.com/). The Vancouver Organizing Committee for the 2010 Olympic and Paralympic Winter Games. 2009. . Retrieved 2009-10-20.

[215] "Official Languages in Canada: Federal Policy" (http://www2.parl.gc.ca/Content/LOP/ResearchPublications/prb0844-e.htm). Library of Parliament. 2009-06-30. . Retrieved 2010-03-26.

[216] "Population by mother tongue, by province and territory" (http://www40.statcan.gc.ca/l01/cst01/demo11a-eng.htm). Statistics Canada. 2005-01-27. . Retrieved 2010-01-19.

[217] "First Official Language Spoken (7) and Sex (3) for Population, for Canada, Provinces, Territories and Census Metropolitan Areas 1, 2001 Census – 20% Sample Data" (http://www12.statcan.ca/english/census01/products/standard/themes/RetrieveProductTable. cfm?Temporal=2001&PID=55535&APATH=3&GID=431515&METH=1&PTYPE=55440&THEME=41&FOCUS=0&AID=0& PLACENAME=0&PROVINCE=0&SEARCH=0&GC=0&GK=0&VID=0&VNAMEE=&VNAMEF=&FL=0&RL=0&FREE=0). Statistics Canada, 2001 Census of Population. . Retrieved 2007-03-23.

[218] "Population by knowledge of official language, by province and territory" (http://www40.statcan.ca/l01/cst01/demo15-eng.htm). Statistics Canada. 2005-01-27. . Retrieved 2009-10-20.

[219] Daoust, Denise (1990). "A Decade of Language Planning in Quebec: A Sociopolitical Overview". in Brian Weinstein. *Language Policy and Political Development*. Ablex Publishing Corporation. p. 108. ISBN 0893916110.

[220] Lachapelle, R (March 2009). "The Diversity of the Canadian Francophonie" (http://www.statcan.gc.ca/about-apercu/ diversity-franco-diversite-eng.htm). Statistics Canada. . Retrieved 2009-09-24.

[221] Hayday, Matthew (2005). *Bilingual Today, United Tomorrow: Official Languages in Education and Canadian Federalism*. McGill-Queen's University Press. p. 49. ISBN 0773529608.

[222] Arnopoulos, Sheila McLeod (1982). *Voices from French Ontario*. McGill-Queen's University Press. pp. 77–81. ISBN 0773504060.

[223] "Aboriginal languages" (http://www.statcan.gc.ca/pub/89-589-x/4067801-eng.htm). *Statistics Canada*. . Retrieved 2009-10-05.

[224] Gordon, Raymond G Jr. (2005) (Web Version online by SIL International,formerly known as the Summer Institute of Linguistics). *Ethnologue: Languages of the world* (http://www.ethnologue.com/web.asp) (15 ed.). Dallas, TX: SIL International. ISBN 1-55671-159-X. . Retrieved 2009-10-06

[225] Fettes, Mark; Norton, Ruth (2001). "Voices of Winter: Aboriginal Languages and Public Policy in Canada". in Marlene Brant Castellano, Lynne Davis, Louise Lahache. *Aboriginal education: fulfilling the promise*. UBC Press. p. 39. ISBN 0774807830.

[226] Russell, Peter H (2005). "Indigenous Self-Determination: Is Canada as Good as it Gets?". in Barbara Hocking. *Unfinished constitutional business?: rethinking indigenous self-determination*. Aboriginal Studies Press. p. 180. ISBN 0855754664.

[227] "The 2006 State of World Liberty Index" (http://www.stateofworldliberty.org/report/rankings.html). State of World Liberty Project. . Retrieved 2007-12-07.

[228] "Doing Business in Canada" (http://www.doingbusiness.org/ExploreEconomies/?economyid=35). World Bank Group. 2010. . Retrieved 2010-02-07.

[229] "The world's best country" (http://www.economist.com/theworldin/international/displayStory.cfm?story_id=3372495&d=2005). The Economist. 2004-11-17. . Retrieved 2010-02-07.

[230] "2005 Environmental Sustainability Index" (http://www.yale.edu/esi/ESI2005_Main_Report.pdf). Yale Center for Environmental Law and Policy, Yale University; Center for International Earth Science Information Network, Columbia University. 2005. p. 4. . Retrieved 2010-02-07.

[231] "Press Freedom Index 2009" (http://en.rsf.org/IMG/pdf/classement_en.pdf). Reporters Without Borders. . Retrieved 2010-02-07.

[232] "Corruption Perceptions Index 2009" (http://www.transparency.org/policy_research/surveys_indices/cpi/2009/cpi_2009_table). Transparency International. . Retrieved 2010-02-07.

[233] "2009 Methodology, Results & Findings" (http://www.alana.org.br/banco_arquivos/arquivos/docs/biblioteca/pesquisas/ 2009-GPI-ResultsReport-20090526.pdf). Institute for Economics & Peace. 2009. p. 10. . Retrieved 2010-06-20.

[234] "Failed States Index Scores 2009" (http://www.fundforpeace.org/web/index.php?option=com_content&task=view&id=99& Itemid=140). Fund for Peace. 2009. . Retrieved 2010-02-07.

[235] Larger number indicates sustainability

[236] "The Global Competitiveness Report 2009-2010" (http://www.weforum.org/documents/GCR09/index.html). World Economic Forum. 2009. . Retrieved 2010-02-07.

[237] "The Economist Intelligence Unit's Index of Democracy 2008" (http://a330.g.akamai.net/7/330/25828/20081021185552/graphics. eiu.com/PDF/Democracy Index 2008.pdf). The Economist. 2008. p. 4. . Retrieved 2010-02-07.

[238] http://www.ocol-clo.gc.ca/docs/e/2004_05_e.pdf

[239] http://www.gc.ca/

[240] http://www.gg.ca/

[241] http://www.pm.gc.ca/

[242] http://www.canadapost.ca/

[243] http://www.cbc.ca/

[244] http://ucblibraries.colorado.edu/govpubs/for/canada.htm

[245] http://www.dmoz.org/Regional/North_America/Canada/

[246] http://www.iccs-ciec.ca/blackwell.html

[247] http://www.cic.gc.ca/

[248] http://www.biographi.ca/index-e.html

Article Sources and Contributors

Colville-Okanagan language *Source*: http://en.wikipedia.org/w/index.php?oldid=375616379 *Contributors*: Bearcat, Giraffedata, Kwamikagami, Mack2, Skookum1, Thesaltflats, Yun-Yammka, 12 anonymous edits

International Phonetic Alphabet *Source*: http://en.wikipedia.org/w/index.php?oldid=377457482 *Contributors*: 100110100, 16@r, 9abdulla, A. Parrot, A12n, ALE!, AVM, Abacavich, Acepectif, Actam, AdiJapan, Aesopos, Aeusoes1, Agent X, Ahoerstemeier, Ajblue98, AjitPD, Akamad, Alison, Allister MacLeod, Allolex, Amire80, Amxitsa, Anarkisto, Anas Salloum, Anchjo, AndonicO, Andrew Dalby, Andyluciano, Angr, Anonymous Dissident, Antandrus, Anthony Appleyard, Antiedman, Aonicc, Apeiron242, Appraiser, Arashi, Arcadian, Ardric47, Arthurian Legend, Athen, Atlantima, AugPi, AxSkov, Az1568, Babbage, Bando26, Beao, Bellenion, Betterusername, Bigwhiteyeti, Bobblewik, Bobo192, Bodigami, Borgx, Bouncingmolar, Branddobbe, Brendaly, Brion VIBBER, Bryan Derksen, Burschik, CJGB, Cafzal, Cakejaron1, Caltas, Cameron Nedland, Can't sleep, clown will eat me, CapitalR, Capricorn42, Carsrac, Cassowary, Causa sui, Ccacsmss, Cgs, Chameleon, Charlesdrakew, Chavash, Chengdi, ChesterMarcol, Chodorkovskiy, Choster, Chris 73, Chun-hian, Ciacchi, Circeus, Closedmouth, Conversion script, Cotoco, CovenantD, Cryptic, CryptoDerk, Cthuljew, Cutefidgety, DRosenbach, DabMachine, DaeX, Dalf, Damian Yerrick, Dan Pelleg, Danenberg, Danlover, Darth Panda, Dato deutschland, Dave Fried, David Latapie, David Marjanović, Dbachmann, Dbenbenn, Dcsohl, DePiep, Denelson83, Denn, DerHexer, Dforest, Diego UFCG, DocWatson42, DopefishJustin, DragonHawk, Drilnoth, Droll, Edward, El aprendelenguas, El estremeñu, Emanuele Saiu, EmilJ, Epitome83, ErWenn, Erebus555, Eric.dane, Erwin, Eslweb, Evertype, Evice, Extransit, Filemon, FilipeS, Firefox-dm, Flapdragon, Fluoronaut, Fresheneesz, Fsotrain09, Funandtrvl, Furrykef, Fvasconcellos, Galoubet, Garik, GauteHK, Gee Eight, Georgia guy, Gerbrant, Gfl87, Gilgamesh, Gilliam, Gioto, Glenn, Godfrey Daniel, Gracefool, GraemeL, Graham87, Grammatical error, Grapelli, Greatgavini, Grendelkhan, Grouse, Grover cleveland, Guaka, Gudeldar, Gyopi, Haham hanuka, Hairy Dude, Hakeem.gadi, Haldraper, Haldrik, Hannes Hirzel, Happenstance, Harryboyles, Haza-w, Henry Flower, HexaChord, Hfastedge, Hippophaë, Hlnodovic, Homunq, Hu, Huhsunqu, Hyacinth, Hypnosnake, Ian Pitchford, Igoldste, Ikiroid, Imz, Ish ishwar, J'88, J. 'mach' wust, JMyrleFuller, JackLumber, Jacobolus, Jacquerie27, James Crippen, Jasper Zanjani, Jdavidb, JeLuF, Jengod, Jennavecia, Jggouvea, Jim10701, Jimp, Jkbjkb, Jnestorius, Joeswork83, John Allsup, John Mark Williams, Jonsafari, Jonverve, Jose77, Jotomicron, Jrockley, Jtir, Juancahoyos, Juicycat, Justified Wikipedian, Kahusi, Kaihsu, Karmosin, Kdammers, Kesac, Killenheladagen, Kingdon, Kinston eagle, Kintetsubuffalo, Kiwibird, Kjoonlee, Knulclunk, Koavf, Krash, Kwamikagami, LLarson, La goutte de pluie, Lacrimosus, Lambiam, Lampman, Landroving Linguist, Largoplazo, Laurinavicius, Lbs6380, Leandrod, LedgendGamer, Lethe, Lfh, Lightmouse, Lincher, Livajo, LjL, Lobbuss, Lotje, Lowellian, LpztheHVY, LukasPietsch, Lumos3, Luna Santin, Lundgren8, Mac, Macrakis, Malafaya, Marco Polo, Mark Dingemanse, Master Conjurer, Matt Gies, Maunus, Mbc362, Mboverload, Mdd, Menchi, Michael Devore, Michael Hardy, Mik01aj, Mikhaela Mittson, Mild Bill Hiccup, Mindmatrix, Minesweeper, Miskwito, Mkouklis, Mlwgsgis1487, Modulatum, Morwen, Mossman fmcb, Moyogo, MuchForgottenLore, Musical Linguist, Musiphil, Mustafaa, Mvjs, Mwalcoff, Mxn, Mzajac, N-true, Ndsg, Neil916, Netrapt, Neutrality, Nickshanks, Nikki, Nneonneo, Nohat, Nposs, Ntsimp, Numbo3, Offenbach, Oghmoir, OldakQuill, Olivier, One half 3544, Ootachi, Oracle of Truth, Ourboldhero, OwenBlacker, Pajast, Paolo Baggia, Paul G, Pauli133, Pconstable, Pcyrus, PenguiN42, Peter Delmonte, Peter Isotalo, Pgan002, Pharaoh of the Wizards, Pi zero, Pigman, Piolinfax, Piotr Gasiorowski, Pipifax, PizzaMargherita, Plankton5005, Pne, Poccil, Potters house, Pt, Ptcamn, Pérez, Quiddity, Qwwqw, R2D2Art2005, R3m0t, RW Marloe, Rabiznaz, Radiant chains, Ran, RandomXYZb, Ravedave, Rayizmi, RekishiEJ, Repku, Rex Germanus, Rich Farmbrough, Rishida, RitKill, RiverDeepMountainHigh, Riwnodennyk, Rjanag, Rjwilmsi, Robert Will, RockMFR, Rodasmith, Ronhjones, RoseParks, Ross Burgess, Sam Hocevar, SameerKhan, Sanmartin, Sannse, Sardanaphalus, Saseigel, Sbrools, SchfiftyThree, SebastianHelm, Seberle, Sebesta, Shimmin, Silsor, Simetrical, Singingkatiebug, Sintonak.X, Skal, Slashname, Sligocki, Slp1, Sonjaaa, Spacevezon, Spencer195, Stalik, Stephan Leeds, Stevertigo, Stripey, Strongbow1800, Sunray, SuperElephant, Suruena, Sw258, TNAWrestlingForeverBaby, TOR, Takuzinis, Tarikash, TarmoK, Tarquin, Tarret, Tassedethe, Taxman, TedPavlic, Tesseran, Tezuni, The Man in Question, The Nut, The Thing That Should Not Be, The Vandal Warrior, The wub, Thegryseone, Thincat, Thnidu, Thrax, Tim Q. Wells, Timpo, Timwi, Tkinias, Tobi aa, Tobias Conradi, Tpbradbury, Trevor MacInnis, Trlkly, Tropylium, Trovatore, Turm, Ultratomio, Umofomia, Untifler, Uriyan, User6854, Vafa Hamidi, Vanished user, Velvetron, VoldermortSmerf, Vystrix Nexoth, Wakuran, Washburnmav, WeijiBaikeBianji, WereSpielChequers, WhatamIdoing, Wikievil666, Wikky Horse, Winston365, Wizardist, Wizardman, Womtelo, Woodstone, Woohookitty, Wrad, Wtmitchell, XJamRastafire, Xcentaur, Xinit, Yes0song, Yupik, Zanaq, Zeimusu, Zhoroscop, Ziiv, Zuloo37, ^demon, ÀrdRuadh21, Ævar Arnfjörð Bjarmason, מראהנייר ירעל, 443 anonymous edits

Salishan languages *Source*: http://en.wikipedia.org/w/index.php?oldid=377322876 *Contributors*: A. Parrot, APT, Altenmann, Aminullah, Andycjp, Angr, Antandrus, Anthony Appleyard, Babbage, Barefact, Billposer, Brindle2009, Bumm13, Burschik, Citicat, Conorobradaigh, DanMS, Decumanus, Deor, DerRichter, Diderot, DopefishJustin, Doradus, Drunken Pirate, Dustinasby, EagleOne, Foonly, Garymorris93, Hapsiainen, Hvn0413, Indon, Ish ishwar, JamesAM, Jlittlet, Jmabel, JorisvS, Katr67, Ken Gallager, Khatru2, Kompar, Ks03, KurtRaschke, Kwamikagami, Lethe, Ling.Nut, Makaristos, Middle Fork, Moxy, Nburden, Ninonino, Oni Lukos, Open2universe, Origamiemensch, Paxsimius, Ptcamn, Raayen, RandomP, Rich Farmbrough, Rosiestep, Ross Burgess, Sassisch, Secretlondon, Selish4life, ShadowDragon, Silverfish70, Skookum1, Sl, Sneakso, Snoyes, Spurius Furius Fusus, Steewi, Steinbach, Sunray, The Man in Question, Themightyquill, Thesaltflats, Tom Lougheed, Trafton, Uanfala, Wikiacc, 63 anonymous edits

Lower Similkameen Indian Band *Source*: http://en.wikipedia.org/w/index.php?oldid=323677863 *Contributors*: Rich Farmbrough, Skookum1

Upper Similkameen Indian Band *Source*: http://en.wikipedia.org/w/index.php?oldid=323665016 *Contributors*: Rich Farmbrough, Skookum1

Westbank First Nation *Source*: http://en.wikipedia.org/w/index.php?oldid=344287681 *Contributors*: Bporrelli, Ckatz, Rakslice, RebaFan1996, Skookum1, Waacstats, 2 anonymous edits

Osoyoos Indian Band *Source*: http://en.wikipedia.org/w/index.php?oldid=348355788 *Contributors*: Skookum1, Tar-ba-gan, Verne Equinox, 1 anonymous edits

Penticton Indian Band *Source*: http://en.wikipedia.org/w/index.php?oldid=323673955 *Contributors*: Madhue, Rich Farmbrough, Sketchmoose, Skookum1, Steam5, 2 anonymous edits

Okanagan Indian Band *Source*: http://en.wikipedia.org/w/index.php?oldid=345805911 *Contributors*: Rich Farmbrough, Skookum1, Themightyquill

Okanagan people *Source*: http://en.wikipedia.org/w/index.php?oldid=340237515 *Contributors*: Arct, Arctur, Aristophanes68, Caknuck, ChrisCork, Colonies Chris, IW.HG, Nk, Richardaedwards, Rjwilmsi, Rosiestep, Skookum1, Themightyquill, 9 anonymous edits

Okanagan Nation Alliance *Source*: http://en.wikipedia.org/w/index.php?oldid=369456966 *Contributors*: Alai, Ka Faraq Gatri, RebaFan1996, Rjwilmsi, Skookum1, Themightyquill

Canada *Source*: http://en.wikipedia.org/w/index.php?oldid=377440109 *Contributors*: $nn00ŦI-I, $yD!, *hollywood*, -- April, ---adam---, -Edwin-, ...adam..., 01011000 (usurped), 0zymandias, 10qwerty, 11.105, 198.103.96.xxx, 1qazxs, 200.191.188.xxx, 23skidoo, 24.70.30.xxx, 2Xtreme21, 334a, 411junkie, 420eryday, 4mehwuzn, 790, 7heesub, 8ung3st, 9.253, A State Of Trance, A bit iffy, A the 0th, A. Lafontaine, AA, ABCD, ACD605, AJP, AJR, AKMask, ARUenergy, ASDFGH, ASOTMKX, Aardvark114, Aaron R, Aaron w, Aaron1541, Aaronlantz, Abhijitsathe, Abonazzi, AbrahamLincoln, Abraxees, Academic Challenger, Acalamari, Ace ventura, Acerperi, Acetylcholinesterase, Achmelvic, Acjelen, Adam Bishop, Adam sk, Adam.J.W.C., Adam1213, Adambro, Adashiel, Addicted04, Adelina and Hannah, Adjusting, Adrian Robson, AdventureGho, Aecis, Aenar, Aesopos, AgarwalSumeet, Ahoerstemeier, Ahuskay, Aim Here, Aiman abmajid, Aiman abmajid@yahoo.com, Aitias, Aivazovsky, AjaxSmack, Ajshm, Akamad, Akanemoto, Aksi great, Alan.ca, Alanharris3, AlbertR, Albertgenii12, Ale jrb, AlefZet, Alensha, Alex756, AlexRampaul, Alexander Domanda, Alexandre.dussault, Alexandrelaplante, Alexcaban, Alexius08, AlexiusHoratius, Alexpappas01, Alexwcovington, Ali K, Alias Flood, Allbrowniesarespecial, Alm93, AlonCoret, Alpdpedia, AlphaTwo, Alphaboi867, Alphachimp, Alphox, Alsadius, Amalthea, Amberrock, Amcfreely, Amgine, Aminovich, Analfuckbaggages, Anand Karia, Anativecantonesespeaker, Andareed, Andem, AndonicO, Andre Engels, Andrew Norman, Andrew Steller, Andrew Yong, Andrew cardz, Andrew0921, Andrewjuren, Andrewpmk, Andrewstark, Andris, Android79, Andrwsc, Andy Marchbanks, Andypandy.UK, Angel2001, Angela, Angelique, Anger22, Angr, AngryParsley, Angryrectangle, Anon1127, Anonymous 57, Anonymous anonymous, Anonymous editor, Anonymousrex, Anowlin, Antandrus, AntarcticPenguin, Anthony Appleyard, Anthony717, Anthonyd3ca, Aolanonawanabe, Ap, Aranel, Arch26, Archanamiya, Archer23, Archer7, Arctic.gnome, Arcuras, Arekku, Argenti1997, Arichnad, Arindamdgp, Arion, Aris Katsaris, ArmadilloFromHell, ArmchairVexillologistDon, ArmchairVexillologistDonLives!, Arnesh, Arolga, AronMathew, Arsha Nos Mondelle, Art LaPella, Artx, Arvind Iyengar, Asad raza5367, Ascidian, Asdquefty, Asenai, AshleyMorton, Ashmoo, Asidemes, Astrotrain, Astrowob, AtheWeatherman, Atlant, Atlantic51, Atorpen, Atrkl, Aude, Aurang, Autocracy, Avala, Avb, Avedomni, Avenue, Avicennasis, Avt tor, Awiseman, AxG, Az1568, Azolnai, BGManofID, Bachrach44, Badhand, Bakersdozen77, Balkania, Bamsucks123, Banes, BanyanTree, Barek, Baristarim, Barneyg, Baronnet, Bart133, BarzaniKurd16, Basketball33man, Batfinkw, BatistareymysteriojohncenatriplehcmpunkHHH, Batman080580, Battlebeast, Bcameron54, Bcarlson33, Bcatt, Bcorr, Bdamokos, Bdiddy, Bearcat, Beerus, Beland, Belligero, Benji Franklyn, Benlumberkid, Bennett, Bensaccount, Benw, Berkut, BernieFan51, Bertilvidet, Betacommand, Beyond My Ken, Bhadani, Bhumiya, Biederman, Big iron, Big juciey, BigCow, BigDunc, Bigfog, BignBad, BilCat, Bilby, Bill37212, Billy5641, Binadot, Bingo bango, Bio1590, Biohazard930, Biwhite2, Bkell, Bkessler23, Bksicoo2, Blackasursowl, Blackjays1, Blahblahblah123, Blazingluke, Blessthishouse, Bletch, Blizzardstep0, Blue520, BlueJaysFan32, BlueLankan, Bluefox, Bluemoose, BnRrain, Bob jim, Bob rulz, Bobanny, Bobblehead, Bobblewik, Bobo Bonnie, Bobo192, Bogdangiusca, BokicaK, Bomac, Bongwarrior, Bonzo the Moon Man, Bookandcoffee, Bookofjude, Boothy443, Bornhj, Bosonic dressing, Bow wow wow, Bowlhover, Boy asunder, Br88, BradBeattie, Bradeos Graphon, Braffit, Brainboy109, BrainyBabe, Brandonha, Brat32, Bratsche, Brendan Moody, Brendan62442, BrendelSignature, BrentS, Breton4real, Brian, Brian Crawford, Brian0918, BrianGV, Brianclegg, Brianjohnson12, Brianporter, Brighterorange, Brindan.b, Brion VIBBER, BritishWatcher, BrokenSegue, Brossow, Bruce b, Brutaldeluxe, Bryan Derksen, BryanG, Bryanjfaber, Bssc81, Btg2290, Bthetford, Bu2m5dgw, Buaidh, Buchanan-Hermit, Buickid, Bull Market, Bully25, Bunny-chan, Burgundavia, Bushcarrot, Buzzfly, Bwilkins, C Hanna, C0C, C12H22O11, CALR, CBM, CDN99, CES, CHEWBACAJC, CIreland, CJ, CMC, CMacMillan, CSIvor, CTCMS, Cabin Tom, Cactus.man, Cadgeo120, Caesarjbsquitti, Cafe Nervosa, CalJW, Calaschysm, Caliper, Calmeida, Calor, Calum Hutchinson, Calvinistsandlutherans, CambridgeBayWeather, Cambyses, Camembert, Camspring, Can't sleep, clown will eat me, Canada Jack, Canadaka, Canadaolympic989, Canadaonline, Canadia, Canadian Bobby, Canadian Copy Editor, Canadian bj, Canadian boy, Canadian popcan, Canadian-Bacon, CanadianCaesar, CanadianElection, Canadianism, Canadianpride, Canderson7, Caniago, Canterbury Tail, Cantus, CapitalSasha, CaptainCanada, CaptainEagle, Carbonite, Caro 08, CarolGray, CarolynParrish, CaseInPoint, Caseam, Caseydk, Casliber, Casper2k3, Catdude, Catgut, Causa sui, Cause of death, Cavenba, Cbb0912, Cbrown1023, Cdernings, Cdollb123, Cedrus-Libani, Cenarium, Censusdata, Cephlapod, CesarB, Chairboy, Chairlunchdinner, Chanting Fox, Charleswin, CharlotteWebb, Chaser, Chatfecter, Che829, Chealer, Check two you, Chem Lady, Cheung1303, Chfbupers, Chillum, Chinneeb, Chippay, Chivista, Chocolateboy, Chodorkovskiy, Chopchopwhitey, Chrisahn, Chrism, Chrisrus, Christopher Parham, Cillas001, Circeus,

Cityhighkid09, Civil Engineer III, CjDMaX, Ckatz, ClEeFy, Clam0p, Clarencedarrow, Clarkbhm, Classicstruggle2, Cleduc, Cloachland, CloudNine, Cloveious, Clq, Clutchcrusher, Cmc0, Cmlau, Cncxbox, Cndcnd, Codylinleyishot, Coffeehood, Cogent, Cogito ergo sumo, Cokoli, Colbrook, Colonel Cow, Commander Keane, Commiessuck, CommonsDelinker, Computerjoe, ComradeRyan, Confiteordeo, ConicProjection, Contributor777, Conversion script, Coolhawks88, Coolkid 297, Copper12, Copperchair, Corticopia, Cortinator, Courcelles, Craggly, Craigston, Craigy144, Crazycomputers, Crazyjoeda, Crewsd, CrnaGora, Croat Canuck, Cruzian, CryptoDerk, Ctjj.stevenson, Ctrl alt delete, CuffX, Curps, D.red.devil, D3dtn01, DCGeist, DGJM, DHickerschmidt, DJ Clayworth, DVD R W, DW, DWMD w, Dabomb87, Dale Arnett, DalminTarnek, Damicatz, Damon96, Dan Koehl, Dan100, Dancingwombatsrule, Daniel C. Boyer, Daniel11, Danielfolsom, Danny, Danshil, Dark falcon, DarkFalls, Darkcore, Darknshadow, Darth Panda, DarthChrist, Dave-ros, Davewild, David Kernow, David Koller, David Levy, David matthews, David winton, DavidSpencer.ca, Davidbessler, Davidcannon, Davidlondon, Davidmintz, Dawn Bard, Dbenbenn, Dbo789, Dbrodbeck, DeadEyeArrow, Dean Elliott, Deathbystarship, Deetdeet, Defenestrate, Deflective, Delldot, Deltazero, Demyx9, Den fjättrade ankan, Dendodge, Denelson83, Dennis Brown, Departmentstoreangel, Derek Ross, Desiphral, Deusfaux, Devourer Kwi, Dharmabum420, Diberri, Diderot, Digfarenough, DigitalC, Digitalme, Dim386, Dimimimon7, Dimimimon8, Dingiswayo, Discospinster, Disinclination, Diskadia, Distal24, Dixitque, Dizla 1, Djd1219, Djinsurgency, Djramone, Djsasso, Dkriegls, Dlohcierekim, Dmz5, Doc glasgow, Docu, Dogru144, Domd Loves ROBLOX, Donteatyellowsnow, Doomstars, Doradus, Dori, Dorvaq, DoubleBlue, Doug Johnson, Doug Trulli, Dowew, Dowlingm, Downtownj, Dpm64, Dr.K., DrKiernan, DrMongol, Draconion devil, Dragon ranch, Dragonfir731, Drbug, Dregganor, Drestros power, Drewgod123, DriveMySol, Drmies, Droll, Dronrob7, Druid.raul, Ds13, DuKot, Dubs69, Duhhitsminerva, Duncachinno, Duncharris, Duomillia, Durin, Durt101, Dustintml, Dvavasour, Dvptl, Dwadejames03, Dynam1te3, Dze27, E Pluribus Anthony, E Pluribus Anthony redux, EBB, EOZyo, ESkog, Eagle4000, EaglesFanInTampa, Eanschuessler, Earl Andrew, Eclecticology, Ed Fitzgerald, Ed Poor, Ed g2s, EdJohnston, Edardna nitsuj, Ede555, Edgar181, Editor18, Edivorce, Edmilne, Edroeh, Eduardo89, Edwy, Efghij, Egil, EhJJ, Ehlkej, Eixo, Ek8, El C, ElKevbo, Elfguy, Elkman, Ellanow, Eloquence, Emadhn, EmmaKateLouisa5, Emufarmers, Englishdumm, Enochlau, Eorlingas, Epsony123, Equazcion, Eric Shalov, Eric119, Ericg, Eroach, EronMain, Erudy, Erwan12, Escriba, Esn, Espantajo, Esteffect, Etams, Etraxler, Eubulides, EugeneZelenko, Evadb, Evans is Awesome, Evercat, Everyking, Everyme, Evil Monkey, Evil saltine, Evolver, EwokMyWeewok, Excirial, Exhaustfumes, ExplodingPineapple, Eyalkatz, Ezhiki, FF2010, FRED, FT2, Facts707, Fakename11, Favonian, Fawcett5, Fcwiki4, Fdp, Feitclub, Felipe Menegaz, Fennellmj, Fenster, Ferhengvan, Ferro Carlotta Monzi Brak, Feydey, Fibonacci, FifthCylon, Figureground, Fire 55, Firehead129, Fireswordfight, Fish 23 23, Fishhead64, Fishtea, Fitzwilliam, Fixedit1980, Flamurb, Flatterworld, Flcelloguy, Floaterfluss, Flosssock1, Floydian, Flubeca, Flyguy649, Fnfd, ForestH2, Formeruser-81, Formeruser0910, Fosnez, Fplax, Fram, Franamax, Franc13, FrankCostanza, Frazzydee, Frea1, Freakinswiit, Freakofnurture, Fredrik, Freemarket, FreplySpang, FreshBulletTime, FreshFruitsRule, Fromgermany, Frostmourne 16, Fry010, Frymaster, Fseeker, Fudoreaper, FueGo, Func, Funnyhat, Future Perfect at Sunrise, Fuzheado, Fvincent, Fvw, G. Campbell, G2bambino, GHe, GNU4eva, Gabbec, Gabrielsimon, Gadfium, Gaius Cornelius, Gaius Octavius Princeps, Galati, Gallisuchus, Gallodannyo, Gamefreek76, Gareth E Kegg, Gareth Owen, Garraisgreat, GarrettRock, Garric, Garrysaint, Garthmyers, Garyskaff23, Gauge, Gavinh9, Gaz, Gazzster, Gbms86, Gcapp1959, Geekboy, Geeoharee, Gegenwind, Gene Nygaard, General Galavan, GeneralPatton, GenuineMongol, Geominers, George The Dragon, George415, Gerdel, Geronimo81, Ggbroad, Gggh, Ghosttowner, Giantgrawp, Giftlite, Gilbert04, Gilliam, Gilliganisland123, Ginascrew, Gjm130, Glen, Glenn, Glenn O' D, Glenn Willen, Gmaxwell, Gnevin, Godefroy, Gogo Dodo, Golbez, Goldenratiophi, Goldfishsoldier, Gomagic, Good Olfactory, GoodDay, Goodguy667, Gopher65, GraemeL, Graham87, GrandfatherJoe, Grandgrawper, Grantsky, Grayshi, GreatWhiteNortherner, Green451, GregRM, Gregalton, Gregory Shantz, Grendelkhan, Griffinofwales, Grimey109, Grizzwald, Grmike, GrooveDog, Ground Zero, Grstain, Grunt, Guanaco, Guettarda, Guilherme Paula, Gundamtidus, Gurch, Guy Peters, Gwernol, Gzornenplatz, H, Haakon, Hadal, Haemo, Hahbie, Hairy Dude, Hajor, HalfShadow, Haljackey, Hallmark, Halthecomputer, Ham, Hamiltonstone, Happenstance, HappyCamper, Happyisgood, Hapsiainen, Hardouin, Harryboyles, Haukurth, Hawkestone, Hayden120, Hayoungs, Hbomb194, Hchrishicks, Hdt83, Head, Headbomb, HeikoEvermann, Heitor C. Jorge, Helios13, Hello4321, Heqs, HereToHelp, Hgrenbor, Hidden2493, Highfields, Highpriority, Highvale, Historianx, HistoryBA, Hockeycraze12000, Homagetocatalonia, Homo sapiens canadensis, Hooverbag, Hoshie, Hottentot, HowardDean, Hu, Hu Gadarn, Huggler, HuntClubJoe, Hunter1084, Hurricane111, Hylaride, Hyperionsteel, Hyyttaa, I am Nicko, I am narcicist, I love val, IHUB.org Founder, Iamcanadian 999, Ian Pitchford, Ian13, Ianvitro, Iapetus, Ibagli, Icairns, Icedevil14, Icestorm815, Ichiroku, Idont Havaname, Ief, Ifnord, Ig0774, Igo4U, Ilikepie2221, Ilovespenserramsey, Iloveweed, Imaginary heroes, Imokru, Improve2009, In God We Trust, Incredible007, Indefatigable, Indianajoes67, Indomaster, InformativeBob, Intangible, Interchange88, Intuitionz, Ipf277, Iran.azadi, IranianGuy, Iridescent, IrishHermit, Irishboy, Irrypride, It allstar, Italianboy10, ItsaMeWallacio, Ivirivi00, Iwtvcanadawiki, Ixfd64, Ixtapl, Izmaster3000, J Di, J.J., J04n, J3wishVulcan, JAKoulouris, JEN9841, JETHRO, JForget, JHMM13, JHunterJ, JJC1138, JLaTondre, JONJONAUG, JQF, JYolkowski, Jacek Kendysz, Jack Cox, Jack2575, Jackmejack, JackofOz, Jackohare, Jackp, Jacky man Toronto, Jacoplane, Jade Knight, Jaegen, Jagged 85, Jallan, JamesR, JamesTeterenko, Jamestown28, Jamielb, Jammy-dodger, Jane xox, Janilson1995, Japeo, Jareand, Jarjarbinks10, Jaxl, Jay Gatsby, Jc3472, Jc8025, Jcart1534, Jcbarr, Jcmenal, Jcuk, Jcw69, Jd.101, Jdforrester, Jean Francois, Jebba, Jeev, Jeff3000, JeffJ, JeffyJeffyMan2004, Jelgie, Jemcgill, Jensboot, JeremyA, Jericho4.0, Jeronimo, JerryOrr, Jetekus, Jew tart, Jezarnold, Jfmacvay, Jgritz, Jguk, Jhynes, Jiang, Jibbajabba, JillandJack, Jim Douglas, JimWae, Jimbo 05247, Jimbo D. Wales, JimboV1, Jimderkaisser, Jimp, Jimpartame, JinJian, Jiy, Jjhcap99, Jjjsixsix, Jkaplan, Jkelly, Jklin, Jnuss, JoSePh, JoanneB, Joel27, Joeldl, Joelf, Joelr31, Joeo c8787, Johann Wolfgang, John Fader, John FitzGerald, John Frink, John Reaves, John Smith M.D., Ph.D, John254, JohnOwens, JohnSankey, Johnleemk, Johnycanal, Joho104, Jokersmoker, Jon.minnette, JonathanDS, Jose77, Joseph B, Joseph Solis in Australia, Josephprymak, Josh.f., Josh619112345267, Joshbuddy, Joshmaul, Joshpascoe, Joshua Scott, Jossi, Joy, Joyous!, Jpdionne, Jpg, Jrbibeau, Jrcrin001, Jringer, Jrv 257, Jtalledo, Jtkiefer, Judge Nutmeg, Judgement, Jules991, Julialovesyou, Junggoo, Juppiter, Jurisprudent, Jusjih, JustN5:12, JustinTSampson, Justinmeister, Jwc4jwc4, Jweiss11, Jwrosenzweig, K3vi0, KFan II, Ka-Ping Yee, Kablammo, Kafziel, Kaguya, Kai Miller, Kaihsu, Kaio-ken x10, Kaisershatner, Kanadiankai, Kanata Kid, Kanthoney, KapilTagore, Karafias, Karl, Karl Dickman, Karukera, Kassia420, Katalaveno, Kavanaugh3, Kbh3rd, Kchishol1970, Keegan, Kel-nage, Kelly Martin, Kelvinc, Kerryboy1, Kesac, Keverich1, Kevin B12, Kevin Taylor, Kevin9999, Kevintoronto, Kevjumba, Kevyn, Keyvoon, Khaerukama'o, Khandoor, Khoikhoi, Khonostrov, Killaboi123, Killerfox, Killerman2, Killsalot11, Kilrogg, Kilter, Kimchi.sg, King George III, King of Hearts, Kingbread, Kingturtle, Kirill Lokshin, Kitch, Kizor, Kjp993, Kkm010, Klaam, Klacquement, Kman543210, Kmsiever, Knave, KnowledgeOfSelf, Knowzilla, Knucmo2, Kokothebread, Kololo4, Konstable, Koopalampudoo, Kotjze, Kotniski, Koyaanis Qatsi, Kozuch, Kralizec!, Kratoz, Krich, Kroeker92, Kross, Kroum, Krun, Krupo, Kryptonian250, Kschembri, Ktr101, Kukini, Kundash, Kungfuadam, Kurieeto, Kuru, Kurykh, Kusma, Kwamikagami, Kwantus, Kwekubo, Kyle sb, Kyle1278, Kyoko, Kyorosuke, Kyuubi9, Kzollman, LOL, La goutte de pluie, LaLa, LaMenta3, Labattblueboy, Lachatdelarue, Lacrimosus, Lakings, Lan360, Landroo, Langston, Lankiveil, Lapsed canadian, Laser brain, Latitude0116, Lauren, Laurentien, Lax4mike, Le temps perdu, LeQuantum, Leadusata, Leafsfan22, Lectonar, Lee Pavelich, Legolas, LegolasGreenleaf, Legopretzel, Leithp, Lemmey, LenW, Lepkio, Leroy jenkinz, Lesouris, Leungli, Levineps, Levram, Lexicon, Lexington50, Liamgibbs, LifeStroke420, Liftarn, Lightdarkness, Lightmouse, Ligulem, Likemike1, LilHelpa, Lilac Soul, Lilpinoy 82, LinaMishima, Ling.Nut, LionKing, Livingdone, Lkjhgfdsa, Llort, Lobes4194, Locos epraix, Lommer, LonelyMarble, Lonewolf BC, Longbranch, Longhair, Longwalkshortpier, Looper5920, Looxix, Lord Voldemort, LordofPens, Loren.wilton, LtPowers, Luatha, Luckienick101, Lucky Strike, Luckyluke, Lucyin, LuigiManiac, Luigizanasi, Luk, Luna Santin, Lupin, Lupo, Lussier, LyndonJohnson, Lynnvallmao, Lzyford, M.C. Brown Shoes, M.nelson, M1ss1ontomars2k4, M3a1xx, M@sk, MCKINLEYROX, MER-C, MJCdetroit, MJR, MKoltnow, MLRoach, MONGO, MTLskyline, Mac99, MacGonagall, MacGyverMagic, Maddytosca, Madmagic, Maedis, Magister Mathematicae, Mahanga, Maijinsan, Mailer diablo, Majorly, Makemi, Malachi is survivin, Malcolm Farmer, Malnourish, Malo, Manbearpig911, Mandel, MarSch, Marc Venot, Marcie, Marcusmax, Mareino, Marek69, Mark Ryan, Mark Zinthefer, MarkGallagher, Markaci, Marknen, MarshallStack, Marskell, Mart98, Martin-C, MartinHarper, Martinp23, Martinwilke1980, Marysunshine, Masalai, Master Jay, Master of Puppets, Mateo SA, Mathieu.gagnon, Mathieugp, Matt Crypto, Matt Deres, Matt Yeager, Mattcrites, Mattgenne, Matthew Samuel Spurrell, MatthewWilcox, Mattingly23, Matttkachu, Mattwilkins, Matx33, Mav, Maverick821, MaxEnt, Maximilli, Maximillion Pegasus, Maximini1010, Maximus Rex, Maxis ftw, Maxmus Rex, Maxwell C., Mayumashu, Mazca, Mb1000, Mbr1983, McRuf2, Mckelveyman, Mdineen, Mdrejhon, Meanie, Medicine man, Meegs, Melander, Melicans, Memo^, Memory9, Menchi, Mendai1991, Mendel, Meneth, Mermaid from the Baltic Sea, Merovingian, Metapotent, Mgiganteus1, Mhking, MiPe, Michael Bramble, Michael Daly, Michael Devore, Michael Dorosh, Michael Glass, Michael Hardy, Michael Voytinsky, MichaelAKautzman, Michalws, Mickey gfss2007, Microbunny, Microsoft 360 GC, Miesianiacal, Migang2g, Mike Dillon, Mike Halterman, Mike Rosoft, MikeCapone, Mikeeatworld2, Mikemikemike4, Mikepedia, Mikerarity, Mikeycanuck, Milkmooney, Millisits, Mindmatrix, Minesweeper, Mingram1, Minority2005, Mir, Miranda, Mirv, MisfitToys, MisterCharlie, MisterSheik, Misza13, Mitchking23, Mkpowers, Mlm42, Mnmazur, Modify, Modulatum, Moe Epsilon, Moeiscool, Moink, Mokwella, Momonono, Momus, Moncrief, MonctonRad, Monegasque, Montblanc.tins, Montoni, Montrealais, MontseBL, Moorehaus, Morganwilliams007, Morwen, Mouse is back, Mousky67, Moxy, Moyogo, Mozart Amadeus Wolfgang, Mozman453, Mr Adequate, Mr Taz, Mr. Lefty, Mr.BOB, Mr.Badlands, Mr.Z-man, MrFish, MrSCBaker, Mrbubbles, Mrchadsexington, Mrdie, Mrmiscellanious, Mrstaple14, Mschel, MuZemike, Muckish, Mudaguin, Muhaidib, Mumble45, Murchy, Murder1, Murphys Law, Music1089, Mxn, My cat is this3, Myleslong, Myrtone86, Mystaker1, Mzajac, N00b pwn3r, NAJohnson, NByz, NCurse, Nachother, Nahallac Silverwinds, Naja Haje, Nakon, Nakos2208, Narcisse, Naryathegreat, Nascar1996, Nat, Natalie Erin, Natalya, Nateirma, Nathanalex, Nathanmccaw, Naturalnumber, Natwatson, NawlinWiki, Nawsum526, Neitherday, Neotenic, Nephtes, Nerguy, Netoholic, Neutrality, NewGuy4, Nfitz, Ng.j, Nhcmedia, Niceley, Nichalp, Nicholas Tan, Nick, Nick125, Nickptar, Nickward1802, NicolasJz, Nidam, Nigersaurus, NightCrawler, Nihiltres, Nikai, Nikkimaria, Niloc, Nirvana888, Nishkid64, Nixeagle, Njc69, Nknight, Nkosi, Nmarritz, Nmpenguin, No Guru, NoIdeaNick, Noitanod, Nokkosukko, Nomi Jones, Nonebrutto, Nooodles, Noozgroop, Nopm, Nords, Noremakk, NorthernChaosGod, NorthernThunder, Norwegianguy, Notforsale101, Notheruser, Novalamatrix, Nsandwich, Ntsimp, NuclearVacuum, Numbo3, Nunh-huh, Nyttend, O1ive, ObiWan353, Oblivious, Ocee, Ogmios, Ohainbhthin, OhanaUnited, Ohnoitsjamie, Old port, OldManRivers, OldRightist, Oldmanboner, Oldsoul, Olivia Jo, Olivier, Omicronpersei8, Onco p53, OneGuy, Ontherox94, Orangefish, Oreo Priest, Orionsky1, Orzetto, Osborg444, Osborne, Otolemur crassicaudatus, Otter Escaping North, Out90, Outriggr, Ovechkinator, OwenX, Oxymoron83, P.T. Aufrette, P4p5, PCM2, PCStuff, PDH, PEAR, PFHLai, PJMIV, PJtP, PKT, PZFUN, Paat, Padraic, Paine Ellsworth, Paint28021, Palefire, Palpatine, Papango, Parent5446, Parkwells, Pat Payne, Patdesjardins, Patman, Pats1, Patstuart, Patycat, Paul Drye, PaulAnthonyDye, Pbehnam, Pblaauw, PcAhRrTiOsN, Pdcook, Pdworkman, PeaceLovingBullets, Pearle, Penser, Pepsidrinka, Peregrine981, PerfectStorm, Persian Poet Gal, Peruvianllama, Peter, Peter Ellis, Peter Fleet, Peter Grey, Peter I. Vardy, Peter Napkin Party, Peter.M.D., Peter243, PeterAKer, PeterisP, Pevarnj, Pewwer42, Pfdstark, Pgan002, Pgecaj, Pgk, Phaedriel, Phenz, Phil Boswell, Phillip J, PhilthyBear, Phoenix2, Phrawzty, Physchim62, PiMaster3, Pianosomething, Picaroon, Piddingworth, PieCam, Pieuvre, Pigman, Pilotguy, Pimpinlt, PinchasC, Pinethicket, Pinkadelica, Pinkville, Pisceesumsprecan, Plasma Twa 2, Plasma east, Plenisphere, Pnatt, Poetaris, Pokrajac, Polaron, Polio, Pollenberg, Pom Sprout, Pomte, Poor Yorick, Poouser, Popadopolis, Popsracer, Porqin, Ppa, Prasi90, Prattlement, Presidentman, Primalchaos, PrincessSade, Pro Grape, Probableprincess, Prodego, Prof.rick, ProfWW, Proteus, PseudoSudo, Psy guy, Puertorico2, Pufflekins, PullUpYourSocks, Purplefeltangel, Pwbk, Pwu2005, Q Canuck, Quadell, QuartierLatin1968, Queen kitten, Quickliger, Quizimodo, Quizimodo (usurped), Qutezuce, Qyd, R-41, RFerreira, RJN, RPlunk, RVD, Rabrams20, Radagast, RadicalBender, RadioKirk, Ramdrake, Rameshfrf, Ran, RandomP, Randomtime, RandorXeus, Randwicked, Randy Johnston, Rarelibra, Rated 619 Superstar, Raudys, RavenStorm, Rawr, Raykak, Rayoflight278, Rayvee2, Rbrewer42, Rddflag, Rdsmith4, Realpop, Reaper X, Recgameboy, Recurrence, RedWolf, Redmarkviolinist, Redthoreau, Redvers, Redwingchamp98, Reedy, Reenem, Regulus marzo4103, Regulus marzo4103@yahoo.com, Reid1867, Remi, RenamedUser2, Renosecond, Ret.Prof, Retired username, RetiredUser2, Rettetast, Rev64, Rev64nes, RexNL, Rhobite, Rholton, Rhyddfrydol, Rhysn, Rich Farmbrough, Richard Harvey, Richardcavell, Richarddd, Richardshusr, Richardvdf, Rick Block, RickK, Ricky@36, Rickyrab, Righteous lies, Riswald, Ritchy, RiverFattieRCool, Riyehn, Rj, Rjayres, Rjensen, Rjwilmsi, Rkt2312, Robbie098, Robchurch, RobertG, RobertHuaXia, Robertsonic1234, Robertsteadman, Robertyoung, Robin Hood 1212, Robin Patterson, Robnorth, RockMFR, Rocker321, Rockies77, Rocksteadyman2, Rodrigogomespaixao, Rogpsro, Romanm, Ron Davis, Ronaldomundo, Rory096, Rosebud13, Rosencrantz1, Ross Burgess, Ross Fraser, Rossgk, Rossnixon, Round55, Roux, RoyBoy, Royalguard11, Rrburke, Rreagan007, Rrius, Rtcpenguin, Ruchi tspl, Rudykruger, RufusW, Rupertslander, Rusl, Rustalot42684, Ruszewski, RxS, Ryan, Ryan Norton, RyanB34, RyanGerbil10, Ryulong, S-Classes, S-Ranger, S0berage, SD6-Agent, SEWilco, SFrank85, SG, SGGH, SNIyer12, SPat, SRE.K.A.L.24, ST47, SUMpTHY, SWAdair, SWBJACMK, Saforrest, Safumbrick, Sagaciousuk, Sagitario, Sahmsiconiol, Sailor for life, Sailujan723,

Image Sources, Licenses and Contributors

Image:IPA in IPA.svg *Source*: http://en.wikipedia.org/w/index.php?title=File:IPA_in_IPA.svg *License*: Public Domain *Contributors*: User:Kjoonlee

File:IPA chart 2005 png.svg *Source*: http://en.wikipedia.org/w/index.php?title=File:IPA_chart_2005_png.svg *License*: Creative Commons Attribution-Sharealike 3.0 *Contributors*: User:Kwamikagami, User:Melroch

File:Phonetik.svg *Source*: http://en.wikipedia.org/w/index.php?title=File:Phonetik.svg *License*: GNU Free Documentation License *Contributors*: User:Fvasconcellos

File:RPGA international.svg *Source*: http://en.wikipedia.org/w/index.php?title=File:RPGA_international.svg *License*: Public Domain *Contributors*: User:Fvasconcellos

Image:Blank vowel trapezoid.svg *Source*: http://en.wikipedia.org/w/index.php?title=File:Blank_vowel_trapezoid.svg *License*: GNU Free Documentation License *Contributors*: User:Angr, User:Moxfyre

File:Cardinal vowel tongue position-front.svg *Source*: http://en.wikipedia.org/w/index.php?title=File:Cardinal_vowel_tongue_position-front.svg *License*: GNU Free Documentation License *Contributors*: User:Badseed

File:Cardinal vowels-Jones x-ray.jpg *Source*: http://en.wikipedia.org/w/index.php?title=File:Cardinal_vowels-Jones_x-ray.jpg *License*: Creative Commons Attribution-Sharealike 2.5 *Contributors*: Ishwar, 1 anonymous edits

Image:Salishan langs.png *Source*: http://en.wikipedia.org/w/index.php?title=File:Salishan_langs.png *License*: Creative Commons Attribution 2.0 *Contributors*: Editor at Large, Huhsunqu, Ishwar, Origamiemensch, RHorning, 2 anonymous edits

Image:Salish-men-tipis-1903.jpg *Source*: http://en.wikipedia.org/w/index.php?title=File:Salish-men-tipis-1903.jpg *License*: Public Domain *Contributors*: Himasaram, Jmabel, Man vyi, Origamiemensch, Uyvsdi, Xnatedawgx, 3 anonymous edits

Image:Okanagan Family Portrait.JPg *Source*: http://en.wikipedia.org/w/index.php?title=File:Okanagan_Family_Portrait.JPg *License*: Public Domain *Contributors*: Themightyquill

File:Flag of Canada.svg *Source*: http://en.wikipedia.org/w/index.php?title=File:Flag_of_Canada.svg *License*: Public Domain *Contributors*: User:E Pluribus Anthony, User:Mzajac

File:Coat of arms of Canada.svg *Source*: http://en.wikipedia.org/w/index.php?title=File:Coat_of_arms_of_Canada.svg *License*: unknown *Contributors*: User:Fibonacci, User:Jeff3000, User:Zscout370

File:Canada (orthographic projection).svg *Source*: http://en.wikipedia.org/w/index.php?title=File:Canada_(orthographic_projection).svg *License*: Creative Commons Attribution 3.0 *Contributors*: Ssolbergj

File:Loudspeaker.svg *Source*: http://en.wikipedia.org/w/index.php?title=File:Loudspeaker.svg *License*: Public Domain *Contributors*: Bayo, Gmaxwell, Husky, Iamunknown, Nethac DIU, Omegatron, Rocket000, 5 anonymous edits

File:Benjamin West 005.jpg *Source*: http://en.wikipedia.org/w/index.php?title=File:Benjamin_West_005.jpg *License*: Public Domain *Contributors*: Arctic.gnome, Emijrp, Gilbertus, Jkelly, Mattes, Mutter Erde, Nonenmac, Rebel Redcoat, Skeezix1000, 1 anonymous edits

File:Fathers of Confederation LAC c001855.jpg *Source*: http://en.wikipedia.org/w/index.php?title=File:Fathers_of_Confederation_LAC_c001855.jpg *License*: Public Domain *Contributors*: Photographer: James Ashfield

File:Canada provinces evolution 2.gif *Source*: http://en.wikipedia.org/w/index.php?title=File:Canada_provinces_evolution_2.gif *License*: GNU Free Documentation License *Contributors*: User:Golbez

File:Canadian tank and soldiers Vimy 1917.jpg *Source*: http://en.wikipedia.org/w/index.php?title=File:Canadian_tank_and_soldiers_Vimy_1917.jpg *License*: unknown *Contributors*: Canada. Dept. of National Defence

File:Oka stare down.jpg *Source*: http://en.wikipedia.org/w/index.php?title=File:Oka_stare_down.jpg *License*: unknown *Contributors*: Shaney Komulainen of Canadian Press

File:Canadian parliament MAM.JPG *Source*: http://en.wikipedia.org/w/index.php?title=File:Canadian_parliament_MAM.JPG *License*: GNU Free Documentation License *Contributors*: Maria Azzurra Mugnai

File:Cansenate.jpg *Source*: http://en.wikipedia.org/w/index.php?title=File:Cansenate.jpg *License*: Creative Commons Attribution 3.0 *Contributors*: User:Mightydrake

File:Medal-Viki.jpg *Source*: http://en.wikipedia.org/w/index.php?title=File:Medal-Viki.jpg *License*: Public Domain *Contributors*: G2bambino, 1 anonymous edits

File:Supreme Court of Canada.jpg *Source*: http://en.wikipedia.org/w/index.php?title=File:Supreme_Court_of_Canada.jpg *License*: Public Domain *Contributors*: Geofrog, Jkelly, Man vyi, Peregrine981, Riba, Skeezix1000, 6 anonymous edits

File:CF-18 Cold Lake Alberta.jpg *Source*: http://en.wikipedia.org/w/index.php?title=File:CF-18_Cold_Lake_Alberta.jpg *License*: unknown *Contributors*: Camera Operator: SMSGT JOHN P. ROHRER, USAFService Depicted:Command Shown: ACC

File:HMCS Regina (FFH 334) 1.jpg *Source*: http://en.wikipedia.org/w/index.php?title=File:HMCS_Regina_(FFH_334)_1.jpg *License*: Public Domain *Contributors*: Avron, Balcer, Dual Freq, Makthorpe, Shipguy, Tabercil

File:Political map of Canada.png *Source*: http://en.wikipedia.org/w/index.php?title=File:Political_map_of_Canada.png *License*: Public Domain *Contributors*: User:Andrew pmk, User:Kaveh

File:Canada-satellite.jpg *Source*: http://en.wikipedia.org/w/index.php?title=File:Canada-satellite.jpg *License*: Public Domain *Contributors*: Anchjo, DrKiernan

File:Canadian Horseshoe Falls with Buffalo in background.jpg *Source*: http://en.wikipedia.org/w/index.php?title=File:Canadian_Horseshoe_Falls_with_Buffalo_in_background.jpg *License*: Public Domain *Contributors*: Ujjwal Kumar

File:STS-116 Payload (NASA S116-E-05364).jpg *Source*: http://en.wikipedia.org/w/index.php?title=File:STS-116_Payload_(NASA_S116-E-05364).jpg *License*: Public Domain *Contributors*: NASA photo

File:Canadian bills2.jpg *Source*: http://en.wikipedia.org/w/index.php?title=File:Canadian_bills2.jpg *License*: Attribution *Contributors*: 293.xx.xxx.xx, Anakin101, Avraham, Cavenba, Churchofpac, DoubleBlue, Fplax, Hammersoft, Io Katai, Jeff3000, Melesse, NAJohnson, NorthernThunder, Royalguard11, ViperSnake151, 8 anonymous edits

File:Nafta.jpg *Source*: http://en.wikipedia.org/w/index.php?title=File:Nafta.jpg *License*: Public Domain *Contributors*: Complex01, Edward, Frank C. Müller, Jkelly, Mattes, Myself488, Shizhao, WikedKentaur, 4 anonymous edits

File:Raven-and-the-first-men.jpg *Source*: http://en.wikipedia.org/w/index.php?title=File:Raven-and-the-first-men.jpg *License*: Public Domain *Contributors*: Michel Teiten http://www.mablehome.com

File:Jackpine.jpeg *Source*: http://en.wikipedia.org/w/index.php?title=File:Jackpine.jpeg *License*: unknown *Contributors*: Tom Thomson (1877–1917)

File:Canada2010WinterOlympicsOTcelebration.jpg *Source*: http://en.wikipedia.org/w/index.php?title=File:Canada2010WinterOlympicsOTcelebration.jpg *License*: Creative Commons Attribution 2.0 *Contributors*: s.yume

File:QuebecCitySum04.jpg *Source*: http://en.wikipedia.org/w/index.php?title=File:QuebecCitySum04.jpg *License*: Creative Commons Attribution-Sharealike 2.5 *Contributors*: Bobak

License

Lightning Source UK Ltd.
Milton Keynes UK
15 February 2011

167598UK00001B/172/P

9 786132 396655